The No-Crowds

Baltic Capitals

Travel Guide

Explore Vilnius, Riga & Tallinn Without the Tourist Traps (Hidden Gems, Quiet Spots & Local Secrets)

Asher. A. Walkley

COPYRIGHT NOTICE

DISCLAIMER

The information provided in this travel guide is intended for general informational purposes only and is based on the author's research, experiences, and opinions at the time of publication. While every effort has been made to ensure the accuracy and reliability of the content, Asher.A Walkley makes no representations or warranties of any kind, express or implied, about the completeness, accuracy, or suitability of the information for any purpose.

Travel conditions, prices, operating hours, safety considerations, and other details mentioned in this guide are subject to change without notice. Readers are encouraged to verify information independently before making travel plans.

The author and publisher are not responsible for any loss, injury, damage, or inconvenience sustained by any person using this guide, including but not limited to reliance on recommendations, directions, or advice provided herein.

FOREWORD

Welcome, lovely traveler, to **The No-Crowds Baltic Capitals Travel Guide**. This guide is born from a passion for exploration and a deep appreciation for the diverse cultures, landscapes, and stories that make our world so extraordinary. Whether you're a seasoned globetrotter or embarking on your first adventure, my goal is to inspire and equip you with the knowledge and confidence to create unforgettable memories.

In these pages, you'll find a carefully curated blend of practical advice, hidden gems, and local insights designed to help you experience **Vilnius, Riga & Tallinn,** authentically and meaningfully. From the busy markets to serene vistas, I have poured my heart into uncovering the essence of this destination and the topic, drawing from my own journeys and meticulous research.

This guide is not just a collection of recommendations—it's an invitation to see the world through curious eyes and an open heart.

As you flip through this book, I encourage you to embrace the unexpected, connect with the people you meet, and let each moment shape your story. Travel is as much about the journey as the destination, and I'm thrilled to be your companion on this adventure.

Happy travels,

Your Travel Writer, Adventurer, and a Blogger

Vilnius Landmarks

Riga Landmarks

Tallinn Landmarks

TABLE OF CONTENTS

WELCOME

Why Travel the Baltic Capitals Without the Crowds?

Most people rush through Vilnius, Riga, and Tallinn like they're on a layover. A few snapshots in the old town, a plate of dumplings, a quick museum, and then off to the next capital. You can spot them by the matching raincoats and slightly glazed eyes. That's not your style—and it's not how these cities want to be seen and explored.

Again, traveling the Baltic capitals without the crowds isn't just possible—it's better. These are cities that reward stillness. The real Vilnius shows itself early in the morning, when the church bells echo across quiet courtyards and the cobblestones are still drying from overnight rain.

Riga comes alive in its side streets, where secondhand bookstores and basement jazz bars hum with life long after the last group tour clocks out. And Tallinn? There's a raw beauty in stepping behind the postcard-perfect old town into neighborhoods where linen flaps on the line and beer gardens fill up with locals, not hashtags.

This guide is about traveling like someone who's been here before—even if you haven't. It's not about skipping every tourist attraction, but about choosing how and when to see them so they feel personal.

You'll find plenty of practical info in the pages ahead—exact tram routes, opening hours that actually reflect reality, and the names of local joints you won't find on page one of search results.

But more than that, this guide is a mindset. It's about not rushing. About pausing before you photograph. About listening. Because the best parts of Vilnius, Riga, and Tallinn aren't necessarily marked—they're felt. And the good news? They're still there. You just have to look a little differently.

Ready? Let's slow it down.

There's a clearheaded joy in seeing Vilnius, Riga & Tallinn at your own pace—when you're the only one leaning over a centuries-old tombstone, or timing your castle stroll before coach-loads roll in. Crowds don't just dilute experiences; they govern schedules, prices, even how close you can get to a window view. Traveling quietly means carving your own moments—those unscripted minutes between guidebook lines.

With this guide, you'll slip into old town backstreets at dawn, linger in neighborhood cafés where locals caffeinate the conversation, and read a skyline like you'd read a story—without distraction.

The Baltic Triangle: What Makes Vilnius, Riga, and Tallinn Unmissable Yet Underrated

All three capitals share medieval lanes, vibrant design, and a thousand years of Baltic grit—but each keeps secrets visitors often miss.

Vilnius

A baroque surprise where golden façades glint at sunrise across the reflective Vilnia River.

Get there early: climb Hill of Three Crosses by 6 a.m. for empty paths and mirror-calm water.

Check the cost: church entry to St. Anne's is €2, St. Peter & Paul's is €3. GPS: 54.6836 N, 25.2903 E.

Insider tip: Take a late-morning detour to Užupis. Walk a couple of blocks north on Paupio Street and discover cheap local pottery shops owned by former Soviet ceramicists—signs read in Lithuanian, so you know it's real.

Riga

Art Nouveau meets market energy. The façades along Alberta iela glow in late afternoon light.

Entry to the Art Nouveau Museum is €5; open 11 a.m.–5 p.m., closed Mon.

- GPS: 56.9520 N, 24.1060 E.

Insider tip: Sidestep the busy central Market and visit the glass-walled Kalnciema Quarter farmers' market on Saturdays—listen for the accordionist who plays at 10:15 a.m., a tradition kept alive by one local family since 2010.

Tallinn

Walled old town with fairytale ice-cream-colored houses. Walk the walls without someone's selfie-stick in your eye.

Town wall walks cost €10; open 10 a.m.–6 p.m.

- GPS: 59.4369 N, 24.7536 E.

Insider tip: Head to Kalamaja just past 9 a.m. on weekdays. The street art collective paints fresh scenes overnight, and you'll catch artists loading their rollers while you sip fog-rolled brew at the local Swedbank café.

How to Travel Differently: A Quiet, Curious, and Slower Way to Explore

This method isn't about ticking boxes. It's thinking about time as a luxury, not a hurdle.

Tips:

- Choose off-peak arrivals. First flights land early enough in all three cities to avoid standard rush. Drag your coffee cart out early—bars open at 7 a.m.
- Walk leisurely between districts. In Riga, stroll from Centrs through Āgenskalns via the railway underpass to discover semi-abandoned Soviet monuments often converted into edgy street art canvases.
- Use pocket-size phrasebooks. Even halting "labdien" in Latvian or "tänan" in Estonian catches locals off guard—in a good way. The café owner may show you the back storeroom or whip out spontaneous card games.

These small moves change engagement: you glide under the radar, and suddenly, your map isn't just eye candy—it's a conversation starter.

Who This Guide Is For: Travelers Seeking Depth, Not Just Selfies

You're not here to count UNESCO sites. You're here to read inscriptions in a dusty church, chart your slowest square in town, pause when the light hits a rooftop just so. You like your coffee taken, not snapped, your cityscape lived, not filtered.

Insider tips:

- Ask the taxi driver for the two-lira cake shop on Vilnius's S. Daukanto Northbank. It's cheap, serves slices that lean toward Lithuanian-style ricotta, and you'll pay in euros or litas without a wince.
- In Riga, the Phillips Chocolate bar inside the historical pink house on the Daugava riverside doesn't look like much—but they make thin salted-caramel bars in summer that come out at 7 pm, gone by 8.
- In Tallinn, join the daily 3 p.m. blue-door walking tour (locally run, name changes weekly). It starts at Freedom Square. No crowds, guaranteed English, and you'll learn a tiny secret that almost nobody includes in guidebooks.

Pro Moves

- Build trust with street vendors: Learn three local words, and you'll get fresh rye sticks or berry juice at cost.
- Start dinner rounds at 5:30 p.m. Weeknight line's vanish, kitchens run warm; servers notice you.
- Use tram windows as moving galleries. In Vilnius, tram 3 passes old Communist apartment blocks with real-time graffiti—sit left for the best view around 6 p.m. Before signs go dark.

Republic of Lithuania, A country in the Baltic Region

Baltic Coast Trail, Latvia

Baltic Station (Balti jaam) in Tallinn

CHAPTER 1

VILNIUS – THE BOHEMIAN BAROQUE BEAUTY

Vilnius is not attention grabbing like Paris or Prague. Vilnius is a quiet, more deliberate place to be. When you are here, you need to slow down and look sideways to see what's actually going on. And that's what makes it so rewarding.

You don't need to be rushing from highlight to highlight while in Vilnius. This city is meant for you to drift, to wander, and to pause. It will allow you one minute you're peeking into a crumbling church courtyard covered in street art, the next you're sipping dark roast in a café where the staff barely glance at tourists.

Vilnius is just being Vilnius—and if you can tune into its pace, you'll find a city that feels honest, unpredictable, and at the same time alive.

This chapter is about traveling differently here: through quieter corners, lived-in neighborhoods, and nearby green escapes where you can hear yourself think. It's the Vilnius Travel Guide for those who want to really feel the place—not just tick it off a list.

Old Town Without the Tour Groups

Vilnius Old Town is one of the largest surviving medieval old towns in Europe, but thankfully, it hasn't turned into a museum piece. People still live here. Real people. That said, most travelers make the same predictable circuit: Cathedral Square, Pilies Street, a quick look at the Gates of Dawn, and done. You can do better.

Start early. Not because of the crowds (they're nothing compared to Paris or Rome), but because Vilnius has a morning rhythm you can only feel if you're out by 8:00 AM. The scent of bread from small bakeries in Vokiečių Street, elderly women walking briskly to Mass at St. Anne's (GPS: 54.6835, 25.2871), and shop shutters lifting slowly.

Head off Pilies Street. Go a block in either direction and the tone changes. Look for the narrow cut-through at Literatų Street. Here, the walls bloom with small tributes to writers—ceramics, iron sculptures, handwritten texts pressed into plaster. No entry fee, no gift shop, just honest art in the open air.

Wander down to Skapo Street (GPS: 54.6834, 25.2878), one of the oldest streets in the city. You'll pass 15th-century buildings still bearing weathered bullet scars from Soviet days. No plaque, no crowd. Just a quiet corridor of layered history.

Then there's the back courtyard of Stikliai Street. Walk through the arches at No. 7, and you'll find a quite little square with faded signage from Jewish glass workshops, a few art galleries, and a tiny wine bar called Somm (www.somm.lt). It doesn't scream for your attention. That's why you should go.

Insider Tips:

- Avoid lunchtime around Cathedral Square. Tour groups tend to cluster here between 12:00–2:00 PM.
- Grab coffee at StrangeLove (GPS: 54.6824, 25.2893). They roast in-house and pull a better espresso than most places in Berlin.
- Visit the Church of St. Theresa at 7:30 AM (GPS: 54.6701, 25.2892). It opens early and you'll have the baroque interior to yourself.

Úzuopis: The Micro-Republic with a Soul

Cross the small bridge over the Vilnia River and you're in another world. Úzuopis is part bohemian art colony, part ideological playground. The locals declared independence in 1997, drafted their own tongue-in-cheek constitution ("Everyone has the right to die, but this is not an obligation"), and appointed a President, Ministers, and even an Ambassador to the Moon.

But it's not all gimmick. Úzuopis is sincere in its weirdness. Artists live here. Ideas are taken seriously. And like all genuine creative communities, it resists packaging.

Start at the Constitution Wall. (Paupio g. 3A, GPS: 54.6789, 25.2960). The text of the Úzuopis Constitution is printed in over 20 languages on mirrored plaques. Spend time reading it—really reading it—and you'll see it's part satire, part manifesto.

Keep walking uphill into the heart of the neighborhood. You'll find courtyards filled with metal sculptures, murals that change every year, and the legendary Angel of Úzuopis statue standing watch over the main square.

Want a real window into the soul of the place? Stop at Úzuokynas, the courtyard of the artist-run gallery Galera (GPS: 54.6781, 25.2985). It's unpredictable—sometimes a quiet place to sketch, sometimes a sculpture park, sometimes a community party spot with vinyl DJs and soup being served from cauldrons.

Eat like a local:

1. Špunka (GPS: 54.6787, 25.2965) for Lithuanian craft beer, no attitude.
2. Paupio Kepyklėlė (bakeshop on Paupio Street, GPS: 54.6786, 25.2958) for pistachio croissants that sell out by noon.
3. One for next-level travelers: Try Keulė Rūkykla (GPS: 54.6774, 25.2942) for BBQ and anarchist murals. It's not for everyone, and that's the point.

Insider Tips:

- Don't just pose under the "Republic of Úzuopis" sign. Talk to someone in the courtyard behind Galera. You'll usually find artists around.
- April 1st is Úzuopis Independence Day. Street theatre, music, passport stamping. Worth planning your trip around.
- Walk along the Vilnia River trail behind Paupio Street for a totally uncrowded view of the neighborhood from the back.

Forests, Hillforts & River Trails Near the City

Here's the thing most visitors don't realize: you can be standing in downtown Vilnius and, 20 minutes later, deep in the forest. No tourist buses, no entry tickets, no plastic-wrapped experience.

Start with Pavilniai Regional Park. It covers over 2,000 hectares of hilly, wooded terrain east of the city. The main entrance is just a 15-minute train ride from the Vilnius railway station to Pavilnys (check train times at www.ltglink.lt, tickets ~€1.20).

The star here is Pūčkoriai Exposure (GPS: 54.6936, 25.3531), a dramatic cliff with views over the Vilnia River valley. There's a hillfort, remains of an old mill, and several marked trails.

Hike the 5km Pūčkoriai Cognitive Trail. It's an easy loop that takes in riverside views, small waterfalls, and old gunpowder warehouses from the 19th century. You'll likely see more joggers and mushroom hunters than tourists.

Belmontas is another good anchor point. It used to be an 1800s-era mill complex, now repurposed into a decent restaurant (yes, touristy, but not awful) and a jumping-off point for longer forest walks. Try the path heading southeast along the Vilnia River toward Markučiai Park—it's flat, quiet, and you might even spot beavers at dusk.

Public Transport Tip: Bus #74 gets you to Belmontas in about 20 minutes from the city center. Or bike it—just follow the paved cycle path along the river starting at the eastern end of Užupis.

Insider Tips:

- Buy snacks at Iki Express (Gedimino Ave. 9) before heading to the park. No food options once you're in the woods.
- Avoid weekends if you want quiet. Locals flood these areas for barbecues.
- Bring bug spray in summer. Mosquitoes here mean business.

Pro Moves:

Want to push beyond the usual traveler track? Here's how to level up your Vilnius experience:

1. Stay in the Šnipiškės district. It's across the river from Old Town, with old wooden houses and a strange industrial/residential mix that feels like nowhere else in Europe. Airbnb options here tend to be cheaper and quieter.
2. Join a Lithuanian-language walking tour with subtitles. Look for events run by Ekskursijos Kitaip (www.kitokiosekskursijos.lt). You'll be paired with locals, not other travelers.
3. Go late. Many churches, like the baroque St. Peter and Paul (GPS: 54.6872, 25.3162), are open until 7 or 8 PM. Go just before closing for an empty, candlelit experience.
4. Vilnius Travel Guide Pro Move: Use the Citybee app to rent an e-bike for a full day. Cheaper than Bolt scooters and more stable on cobblestones.

Vilnius Vilnia

CHAPTER 2

RIGA – EUROPE'S BEST-KEPT CAPITAL SECRET

There's a moment when Riga sneaks up on you. Maybe it's in the early light filtering across the Daugava River, or the way a jazz band spills out onto a side street behind a peeling wooden house. Riga isn't loud about its greatness—but if you're paying attention, it hits hard. This isn't the kind of capital that's overrun or overly curated. Riga still feels lived in, layered, and a little contradictory in the best way.

For travelers who'd rather wander than queue, Riga delivers. You just need to know where to look—and when.

The Real Art Nouveau District

Riga's architectural ego is well-earned—but not where you might expect. The postcard-perfect Alberta iela gets all the attention, but the city's real charm unfolds in the quieter corners of its Art Nouveau neighborhoods, where no one's posing, and the drama is all in the facades. This is where to start—early, slowly, and with your eyes up.

How to explore without dodging selfie sticks

Let's get this out of the way: yes, Riga is often cited as having the highest concentration of Art Nouveau buildings in the world. Yes, Alberta iela is the famous one. And yes, it's where most people stop—and that's exactly the problem. That single street, beautiful as it is, gives you about 10% of the picture. The real beauty spills across quiet, residential blocks where locals still carry groceries and smokers lean out of windows beneath stone lion heads.

To really see Riga's Art Nouveau, start early—before 9am if possible—on Elizabetes iela, near the corner with Antonijas iela (GPS: 56.957364, 24.104301). From there, you can drift northwest toward Strelnieku iela and Vilandes iela, following the ornate facades that get more intricate the deeper you go. Pay attention to doorways, wrought iron balconies, and absurd details like owls, sphinxes, or screaming faces—Riga's architects had a flair for the dramatic.

If you're up for a smart detour, skip the pricey (and underwhelming) Art Nouveau Museum and head instead to Jūgendstila Centrs in the Riga Art Nouveau Center at Alberta iela 12. It's better curated and gives you context without feeling like homework. Entry is €9; open Tuesday–Sunday, 10am–6pm (closed Mondays).

Insider Tips:

- Many Art Nouveau buildings are now embassies or apartment blocks. Some allow courtyard access—don't be afraid to peek in respectfully if the gates open.
- Want the money shot without tourists? Shoot Alberta iela from the southern end right around 8:15am.
- The Art Café Sienna (Strēlnieku iela 3) does strong espresso and has a leafy terrace locals actually use. Perfect base before or after your walk.

Markets, Microbrews & Mežaparks

If the Art Nouveau quarter is all about ornament and aesthetics, this next stretch of Riga is about rhythm—daily life, big appetites, and green space where the city breathes out. Here's where the raw energy of the Central Market meets the calm of pine forests and lazy lakeside afternoons. Come hungry, leave unhurried.

Central Market early morning circuit

Riga's Central Market isn't your Instagram-friendly food hall. It's vast, a little chaotic, and very real. Housed inside repurposed Zeppelin hangars (yes, really), it sprawls across five halls and dozens of outdoor stalls. Early morning—ideally before 9am—is when it's at its best. Vendors are more relaxed, and you'll dodge the cruise-ship day trippers.

Start in the Fish Pavilion (GPS: 56.943339, 24.114423). There's a briny intensity to the place—rows of smoked fish, caviar tins, and vendors shouting prices. Then cut through to the Produce Pavilion, where everything smells like dill and sour cherries. If you're assembling a picnic, this is the time. Latvian cheeses, thick rye, dried sausage, and honeycomb are easy wins.

Once you've stocked up, hop tram #11 from the nearby Centrāltirgus stop to Mežaparks (GPS: 56.998819, 24.128611). It takes 30 minutes and feels like a shift in dimension. Mežaparks is Riga's green lung—a forested, lake-threaded neighborhood where locals jog, picnic, and ignore their phones. Rent a bike or just walk. The air smells like pine and lake water.

Insider Tips:

- Bring cash. Many Central Market vendors don't take cards.
- At Mežaparks, head to Īšezers Lake. The pier behind Cafe Vigvam (GPS: 57.001260, 24.130447) is rarely crowded.
- Tram #11 still uses old-school ticket punchers. Buy a €1.50 ticket at a Narvesen kiosk in advance.

Soviet Ghosts & Wooden Houses

Now for Riga's quiet underside. Just beyond the polished center, neighborhoods like Maskavas Forštate and the wooden quarters to the southeast feel slower, heavier—thick with memory and contradiction. These aren't the places that show up in brochures, which is exactly why they're worth your time.

Maskavas Forštate, Latgale Suburb, Riga, Latvia

Riga's other side: Maskavas Forštate and the silent stories of wooden neighborhoods

Most visitors stick to Riga's polished center. Few ventures across the tracks into Maskavas Forštate, Riga's Moscow District. It's quieter here. Grittier. And strangely beautiful in its decay.

Soviet-era housing blocks loom beside crumbling 19th-century wooden homes, and the mix tells a story that hasn't been glossed over.

Start your walk at Lāčplēša iela 119 (GPS: 56.948172, 24.141992) and drift southeast. You'll pass through quiet residential streets where Orthodox churches and overgrown courtyards speak to the district's deep Jewish and Russian heritage. The Holocaust Memorial on Gogola iela is worth a moment of silence. From there, walk toward Lastādija, an evolving artist district that's finding its footing without being cute about it.

Krāslava, Lāčplēša iela

These wooden houses are the soul of Riga. Built mostly in the late 1800s and early 1900s, many are in disrepair—but that's part of their draw. They creak. They lean. They remind you that cities age, too. Locals call them "koka mājas," and the ones around Kalna iela and Mazā Krasta iela are especially haunting late in the day.

Insider Tips:

- Don't wander this district after dark solo unless you know where you're going. It's not dangerous per se, but it's not polished either.
- Some of the best photos come from second-story tram windows. Tram #7 and #3 both roll through this part of town.
- For a low-key lunch, try the canteen-style LIDO Krasta just across the river. It's retro in a way that works.

Pro Moves:

1. Want Riga without the noise? Travel midweek, avoid festivals, and base yourself outside Old Town— Āgenskalns is a smart, tree-lined neighborhood with strong cafés and no tour groups.
2. Digging into culture? Skip the predictable art museums and head to the Zuzeum Art Centre (GPS: 56.943496, 24.117889). It's industrial, modern, and not afraid to take risks. Entry is €7, open daily except Mondays from 11am– 7pm.

3. Is coffee more your thing? The best in town is at MiiT Coffee (Lāčplēša iela 10). They roast their own beans, serve a solid vegetarian lunch, and the vibe is strictly locals catching up, not laptops and lattes.
4. And one last word: Riga rewards patience. It may not dazzle in an hour, but give it a few days, go off-script, and it starts revealing itself—block by block, face by face, pastry by pastry.

A great and another European capital—it's a place you can actually get to know fast.

Lāčplēša iela

CHAPTER 3

TALLINN – MEDIEVAL WALLS, MODERN EDGES

Tallinn is one of those places where the past and present don't just coexist—they collide, spin around, and end up clinking beer mugs together. In this chapter, we're zeroing in on what makes Estonia's capital so addictive: the layers.

One moment, you're standing in a shadowed alleyway that looks like it hasn't changed since 1490. Blink, and you're inside a minimalist coffee bar pouring oat flat whites with beans roasted around the corner. This chapter is about those contrasts, but more importantly, it's about showing you the parts of Tallinn that people don't always talk about. The towers without lines.

The old town views without crowds. The warehouse neighborhoods that Estonians have quietly turned into cultural gold. We're also heading out of town for a breath of coastal air and a taste of Estonia's wilder side. Ready to move beyond the basics?

Secret Corners of the Old Town

Everyone sees Tallinn's Old Town. Not everyone sees it right.

Yes, there are groups trailing behind tour guides holding up fish-on-a-stick signs, but there are also spaces in the Old Town where the noise drops out and the history hums differently. If you walk with intent—and a little curiosity—Tallinn still rewards you with moments that feel all yours.

Start at Laboratooriumi Street. It runs along the inside of the northern wall, and unlike the more polished Viru Gate area, it has a rough, almost forgotten texture. You'll find cracked stone, ivy-covered walls, and parts of the medieval fortifications that feel unsupervised in the best way.

About halfway along, climb the Hellemann Tower (3€, open daily 10am–6pm in summer). You might have to ring a bell to get in. Inside, narrow staircases lead to parapet walks that curve above the street with near silence. The view down to the red rooftops? Crisp and uninterrupted.

Head next to the Patkuli viewing platform (GPS: 59.4399, 24.7437). Most tourists go to Kohtuotsa, which is fine if you want a selfie line. But Patkuli is better for quietly taking it in: St. Olaf's spire, the fat round bastions, the Baltic shimmer. Come at sunset with a local beer and a sense of patience.

Then there's the Danish King's Garden (Taani Kuninga Aed). It sounds like a Disney-fied bit of medieval history, but it's surprisingly moody. During the day, you might find a harpist playing beneath the arches. But the real draw is climbing up Lübberök Tower (entry 5€; open 11am–7pm May–Sept). This tower is frequently missed. Inside: old weapons, wax knights, and a high view that actually lets you peek into cloisters most people never see.

Insider Tips:

- Skip the Town Hall interior unless you're deep into medieval municipal politics.
- The city walls near Nunna Tower often let you walk sections without supervision—check for open gates.
- Maiasmokk Cafe (Pikk 16) is the oldest cafe in Tallinn and can be a circus up front. Slip upstairs to the marzipan room for some breathing space and a quiet coffee.

Tallinn kohvik Maiasmokk

Kalamaja & Telliskivi: Urban Cool Without the Noise

Telliskivi Tänav (Tallinn)

Once a sleepy fishing district, Kalamaja now walks the line between laid-back and sharp-edged. You don't come here for marquee sights. You come for the feeling that Tallinn is figuring itself out in real time.

Start at Telliskivi Creative City (Telliskivi 60a, GPS: 59.4393, 24.7317). It's a former industrial zone turned design hub, but without the hipster overload. Yes, there are neon signs and espresso bars, but there's also artists screen-printing in open garages and Estonian kids playing football between murals.

One anchor is Fotografiska Tallinn (entry 12€; open daily 10am–11pm). Don't skip the rooftop terrace—the view isn't high, but it gives a rare horizontal look at Tallinn's layered skyline. For lunch, try Peatus, a restaurant in an old Soviet train car. It sounds gimmicky, but the burger and Baltic herring plates are local favorites for a reason.

Go through Kalamaja's wooden house district—the streets around Valgevase and Kaarli pst still feel residential, with bikes on balconies and kids chalking the sidewalks. Stop at Ristikheina Kohvik for cake and coffee (open daily 9am–9pm), especially in the late afternoon when locals slide in for post-work treats.

If you're around on a Saturday, Balti Jaama Turg (the central market near the station) is a must. Head to the second floor for vintage Estonian military coats and handmade wool socks. Downstairs, the smoked fish vendors will let you sample first. Cash is handy, but most stalls take card.

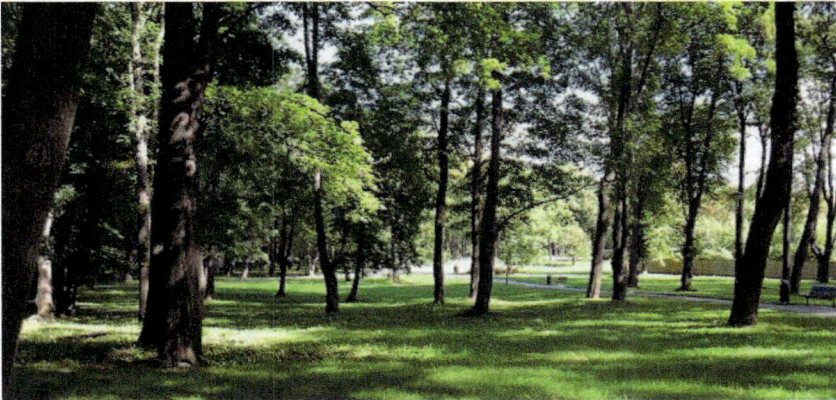

Tallinn, Kalamaja kalmistu

Insider Tips:

Fotografiska tickets can be bundled with Telliskivi gallery events—ask at the info desk.

The best pastries in the area? Karjase Sai (Telliskivi 2).

For a quieter beer garden than the rowdy Old Town pubs, try Põhjala Tap Room (Peetri 5) near the waterfront—it's all local brews with sea breeze.

Day Trips to Lahemaa & Paldiski

Tallinn's great, but Estonia's soul is in its forests, bogs, and open sky. Luckily, you don't need a full road trip to get a taste.

Lahemaa National Park (GPS: 59.5656, 25.6398) is an hour east. Rent a car for the day or join a local tour (Prangli Travel runs solid small-group options from 75€ per person). What you get: ancient pine forests, coastal trails with no one on them, and manor houses like Sagadi and Palmse that still creak with history. The Viru Bog Trail is the easiest intro (3.5km round trip; boardwalk the whole way). Go early and you'll have the place to yourself, mist and all.

Stop at Altja fishing village for lunch—the taverna (Altja Kõrts) does smoked fish platters with black bread and horseradish that hits just right after a walk. If you're self-driving, parking is free and easy, and signage is solid.

On the opposite coast, Paldiski (GPS: 59.3567, 24.0577) feels like the edge of the world. Once a closed Soviet submarine base, it still has that haunted feeling. But that's part of the draw. The Pakri cliffs are 25 meters high and drop dramatically to the Baltic. Walk the bluff trail, then check out the lighthouse (entry 5€, open 11am–7pm summer only). It's one of Estonia's tallest and the view, if it's not fogged in, is sweeping.

For Soviet the history buffs, the crumbling garrison buildings around town are still standing. They're not preserved tourist sites—they're just there. Quiet, eerie, and real.

Insider Tips:

- Viru Bog has a tower halfway in—climb it for the best morning light.
- In Paldiski, the little kiosk near the train station sells surprisingly good smoked cheese pastries.
- The Tallinn–Paldiski train (about 1 hr, 4€ one-way) is functional and atmospheric—go in the morning to catch the market buzz in Paldiski.

Pro Moves:

- Don't cram all three into one day. Do Old Town and Kalamaja on foot with breathing room. Then save a full day for Lahemaa or Paldiski—or both if you have wheels.
- Want even more solitude? Visit Lahemaa on a weekday. Weekends bring day-tripping Tallinn locals.
- In summer, Tallinn's sun doesn't set until after 10pm. Use that golden hour to see places most people clear out of by 7.

This is Tallinn at its richest: layered, local, and laced with contrast. You just have to know where to look—and when to go.

Lahemaa Viru

CHAPTER 4

GETTING AROUND THE BALTIC CAPITALS WITHOUT STRESS

Travel between Vilnius, Riga & Tallinn is no longer a guessing game of long bus rides or pricey flights—it's now neatly woven into a network of trains, roads, and occasional flights.

Let us get into the most practical breakdown of how to move smoothly between the capitals, cross borders like a local, and choose the right mode of transport to suit your pace and style.

Baltic Shuttle Bus in Estonia

Train, Bus, or Car? The Real Transportation Options Broken Down

Let's be blunt: trains in the Baltics aren't the smooth, high-speed dream you might hope for. They're improving—Lithuania's rail network is the most modern of the three—but still not ideal for hopping capital to capital. You won't find a direct train linking Vilnius, Riga, and Tallinn. That job falls to the intercity buses, which, despite sounding like a compromise, are surprisingly excellent.

Buses: Your Best Bet Between Capitals

Forget what you think you know about long-distance buses. Operators like Lux Express and Ecolines have raised the game with roomy seats, personal entertainment screens, Wi-Fi that actually works (most of the time), and air conditioning that doesn't freeze you to death. Even the toilets are clean—yes, really.

Vilnius to Riga: 4 hours, €18–€25, 6–10 departures/day.

Riga to Tallinn: 4.5–5 hours, €20–€28, frequent daily departures.

They run like clockwork. No check-in lines, no faff. Just show up 10–15 minutes early, scan your QR code, and you're good.

Main departure points:

- Vilnius Bus Station (GPS: 54.6709, 25.2843)
- Riga International Coach Terminal (GPS: 56.9444, 24.1139)
- Tallinn Bus Station (GPS: 59.4271, 24.7682)

Operating hours: 05:00–23:00 depending on route. Book at www.luxexpress.eu or www.ecolines.net

Insider Tips:

1. Book a Premium or Business class ticket on Lux Express for a wider seat, quieter cabin, and power sockets that actually charge your device past 20%. Worth the extra €6.
2. Bring your own snacks. The onboard vending machine exists, but it's more of a "just in case" safety net than a satisfying meal option.
3. Avoid the back row. It's near the toilet, which means less legroom and the occasional whiff of reality.

Trains: Limited, But Useful in Lithuania

Within Lithuania, the Lithuanian Railways system (LTG Link) is modern, reliable, and cheap.

- Yes, Vilnius to Kaunas is Easy.
- While to Klaipėda is a scenic ride.
- Vilnius–Kaunas: 1.5 hours, €6.
- Vilnius–Klaipėda: 4 hours, €15.

But between the Baltic capitals? No go. There's currently no direct international train between Vilnius, Riga, and Tallinn. A new Rail Baltica high-speed line is in development and scheduled to link all three cities in the next few years, but as of mid-2025, it's still in construction limbo.

Insider Tip: If you're day-tripping from Vilnius to Kaunas, take the early morning train (around 7:00am). You'll avoid the local commuter crush and snag a window seat for the green rolling countryside.

Car Rentals: Freedom with Caveats

Renting a car in the Baltics can be tempting—especially if you're eyeing off-the-path spots like Sigulda's castle valley, Estonia's Soomaa National Park, or Lithuania's Hill of Crosses. Roads are decent, traffic is light outside the capitals, and border crossings are painless (thank you, Schengen).

But here's the catch: cross-border drop-off fees can be sneaky-high. Renting in Vilnius and dropping in Tallinn? Expect an extra €150+ if you don't read the fine print.

Rental advice: Stick to reputable names (Hertz, Sixt, Europcar) and double-check if the vehicle is allowed to cross borders. Some budget outfits will deny claims if you drive into Latvia or Estonia without notifying them first.

- Average daily rental: €35–€50/day
- Fuel price: ~€1.65/litre (June 2025)
- Documents: EU driving license or International Driving Permit if from outside EU.

Insider Tips:

- Want to avoid the one-way drop-off fee? Plan a loop: Vilnius → Riga → Tallinn → Pärnu → back to Riga → Vilnius. It adds a couple of scenic detours and saves you €150 in rental surcharges.
- Google Maps is mostly reliable, but Waze handles unexpected roadworks better, especially in Riga's outer suburbs where detours pop up unannounced.

Border-Crossing Tips and Lesser-Known Routes

Crossing borders in the Baltics is like moving between regions, not countries. No passport checks, no customs lines—just seamless driving or riding through. But there are smarter ways to plan the transitions.

The Scenic Route: Vilnius to Riga via Daugavpils

Instead of the direct Vilnius–Riga bus, consider routing through Daugavpils, Latvia's second-largest city. It's not flashy, but its Soviet architecture and peculiar vibe make for a very different Baltic experience. Stay a night if you're the curious kind.

- Vilnius to Daugavpils: ~2.5 hrs by train (€9)
- Daugavpils to Riga: ~3.5 hrs by bus (€12)

The Coastal Route: Riga to Tallinn via Pärnu

Break up the journey between Riga and Tallinn with a relaxing stop in Pärnu, Estonia's laid-back "summer capital." Think beaches, seaside cafés, spa hotels, and a splash of local art.

- Riga → Pärnu: ~2 hrs by bus (€10–€12)
- Pärnu → Tallinn: ~2 hrs by bus (€10)

Ideal for travelers who prefer a slower pace or an overnight by the water.

Insider Tip: If you're using buses for these detours, check www.tpilet.ee (Estonia's national ticket platform) and www.1188.lv (Latvia's transport portal). They're more up-to-date than the Google algorithm.

Local Airlines vs. Land Travel

Here's the bottom line: flights between the Baltic capitals are a bad use of time and money unless you're connecting onward to another country.

Riga to Vilnius or Tallinn by air: Takes 50 minutes in the air, but at least 3.5 hours door-to-door with airport transfers, security, and delays.

Direct flights Riga–Tallinn: ~1 hr, €80–€120 one-way (checked bag often cost extra)

Local carriers like Air Baltic and NyxAir do run these routes, but unless you're short on days or your return flight demands it, skip the planes.

When flights do make sense:

- Connecting from Tallinn to Stockholm, Copenhagen, or Helsinki
- Need to get from Vilnius to Berlin fast
- When tou're catching a tight international flight with no rail/bus workaround

Insider Tips:

Use Riga International Airport (RIX) as your main hub. It's the largest in the Baltics and often has better fares than Vilnius or Tallinn—even for non-direct routes.

If you must fly between Baltic capitals, pack ultra-light and avoid checked luggage. It's the only way flying beats the bus timewise.

Pro Moves: Next-Level Advice for Getting Around

Mix transport styles. Take the bus between capitals, rent a car for countryside exploring, then ditch it before re-entering the next city. It's the best of both worlds—low stress and full freedom.

Use local apps. For city-level transit:

- Vilnius: Trafi (for real-time bus tracking)
- Riga: Rīgas Satiksme app or Mobilly for ticketing

Tallinn: Pilet.Ee For Tram/Bus Schedules And QR Tickets

- Look for combo tickets. Some regional buses and museum discounts are bundled—especially in Estonia. Ask at the Tallinn Tourist Info Center for current bundles (GPS: 59.4365, 24.7453).
- Avoid rush hours in each city—especially Friday afternoons when locals flee to the countryside. Leave before noon, and you'll miss the traffic snarl.

Getting around the Baltics isn't about hacking the system, it is more about knowing which options actually work on the ground. Buses win for city-to-city comfort and price, trains shine within Lithuania, and a rental car unlocks the lesser-seen side of the region—just be smart about when and where. Use this guide, and you'll avoid the usual headaches and move through Vilnius, Riga, and Tallinn like you've done this before.

CHAPTER 5

WHERE LOCALS GO – PARKS, LAKES, AND PICNIC SPOTS

City centers are great place to find nice parks, lakes, and picnic spots—but the real relaxation in Vilnius, Riga & Tallinn happens where locals sneak off for clarity, calm, or a lazy afternoon in the grass. You've seen a bit; let's show you where people actually go to breathe. These are less-marketed, more-lived-in outdoor escapes that feel like a reset button for your senses.

Best Outdoor Escapes Inside and Just Outside Each Capital

Feel the air shift on a slow walk through Vilnius's Vingis Park. It's the city's green lung, a soft blanket of grass and pine where families picnic and joggers lap the main trail. Locals don't bother with the manicured paths around Užupis; they spread a blanket under the willow-thin rows near the river. GPS: 54.6833, 25.2486. Open 24/7. No entry fee.

On the opposite side of Vilnius Old Town, Kalnų Parkas (Hill of Three Crosses hill) delivers quiet forest trails that connect to panoramic city views. Go early, around 7 a.m., and the light hits the city rooftops just right. The café at the top opens 9 a.m.– 8 p.m. (offering espresso for about €2) and locals' line up fast for the first brew.

Riga's secret spot? Mežaparks does more than host concerts. Beyond the stage lies a bog boardwalk—62 hectares of marsh and spruce where the air turns softer. Accessible by tram 11 (last stop) at GPS 56.9860, 24.1356, it opens at 6 a.m. and shuts the gates at 10 p.m. Free to enter; small café near the lake sells local rye bread sandwiches for €3.

In Tallinn, skip crowded Kadriorg and go west to Nõmme Forest Park. Pine-scented trails slope down toward the old Nõmme train station (GPS 59.3790, 24.7140). It feels like a countryside village inside the city. Weekdays, it's nearly empty at dawn. No admission. Coffee truck pops up on weekends from 8 a.m.; espresso + pastry ~€4.

Just outside each capital, fresh corners await. From Vilnius, a 30-minute bus ride (Line 3G) lands you at Liepkalnis Recreation Area (GPS 54.6679, 25.1010), where the artificial lake and grassy slopes draw more locals than tourists. Small entry fee is €1.50. Bring your own towel—chairs rent for more.

A short drive from Riga, Daugmale Island near the Daugava delta offers quiet marsh trails and spots for a lunch you didn't know you needed. Take bus 26 to Doles sala ferry zone; cross at 9 a.m. (runs until dusk). No fee. Carry water; the only café is 45 minutes round-trip.

From Tallinn, head 25 km south to Kõnnu Bog on the train to Türi; get off at Keava station. A boardwalk snakes over the sphagnum—a cool 12 °C under the trees. Entry's free; no facilities. Bring snacks.

Insider Tips for Outdoor Escapes:

In Vilnius, bring a frisbee to Vingis Park early—locals love an impromptu game, and you'll get invited.

In Riga, fetch a fresh local rye roll from Mežaparks's small café and sit by the lake—Riga's early sun hits the boardwalk just right.

In Tallinn, catch the 6:30 a.m. train to Nõmme Forest—empty trails, birds dominating airspace, and the nearby deli opens at 7 a.m. for coffee and pastry.

Secret Beaches and Quiet Lakes

Urban beaches can be noisy. Let's show you where locals really go when they need calm water, not crowded sand.

In Vilnius, Lake Žalieji Ežerai (Green Lakes) is a ring of three small lakes 10 km north of the city center. Catch bus 1G from Žalieji Ežerai stop, ride 25 mins (single ticket ~€1.20).

Locals pick the easternmost shore; fewer families, more anglers. Noon–4 p.m. is the peak shade time. Lifeguards on weekends. Café kiosk sells ice cream from €1.50.

Closer in, Balsiai Quarry (GPS 54.7540, 25.2120) is a former gravel mine turned freshwater melee—good for early-afternoons when the sun heats the water, but tourists don't know it. Take the 17 buses from Žirmūnai Bridge stop (20 mins). No fee; no facilities—pack water and snacks.

Lake Ummis is on Ķīpsala Island, just across the bridge from Riga's Old Town. You can walk there in about 30 minutes, or take bus 26 from the city center, which drops you near the quieter south shore (GPS: 56.9510, 24.0870). If you're driving a rental, there's parking nearby.

It is a low-key local spot, mostly known to people who live in the area. The water is shallow and clean, and you'll often see locals standing knee-deep, cooling off on warm days. Around 5 p.m., the light softens into a golden haze—nice if you're planning to relax, take photos, or just sit by the edge.

There aren't any food stands or cafés nearby, so bring sandwiches or something to drink if you're planning to stay a while. It's not a destination with big signs or crowds—just a quiet pocket of water where Riga slows down for a bit.

Out of town, Lake Āraiši is a 40-minute drive north. Cooler and deeper, old island fishing huts turned picnic huts, rentable for €4/hr from 10 a.m.–8 p.m. Circle the small island via footbridge. Bring a sweater—the wind picks up fast.

Most visitors know about Stroomi Beach, but if you ride tram 1 just one stop further, you'll land at Pelgurand (GPS: 59.4435, 24.7280)—a quiet area where locals unwind, especially on warm weekdays after 5 p.m.

It's not as sandy as Stroomi, but the sea breeze is stronger, the vibe more relaxed, and the crowd noticeably smaller. By evening, the dunes come alive with small cookouts. Locals grab €4 grills from a pop-up stand, lay out sausages, and use the free charcoal provided near the shore.

No big signs, no tourist rush—just a casual, everyday beach scene with a **Tallinn twist**.

For a lake fix near the city, Lake Harku (GPS 59.4320, 24.6060) is 8 km west. From Balti jaam, bus 27 goes straight. This is slow-boat locals' domain—kayaks, fishing boats, families picnic. No entrance fee. Café behind the beach opens 8 a.m.–9 p.m.; coffee ~€3, sandwiches around €5.

Insider Tips: Beaches & Lakes Like a Local

1. **Vilnius** – Head to Balsiai Quarry on Friday afternoons. It's when locals show up with grills, music, and time to hang out. Still, plenty of space to spread a towel or claim a shady spot.
2. **Riga** – At Lake Ummis, bring your own float or air mattress. Locals often drift across in swimsuits or raft-hop with friends. It's relaxed, friendly, and easy to join in without saying much.
3. **Tallinn** – Try Pelgurand after 8 p.m. in summer. The sun drops low, the breeze cools down, and most swimmers have packed up. The light turns golden—it's the quietest, most beautiful time to be there.

When to Go for Solitude

Timing your outdoor sessions matters as much as picking the spot. Here's the best of the day, week, and season.

Early Mornings (6–9 a.m.)

Weekdays, none of these places feel public—they feel private. You'll meet joggers, a few dog walkers, and that's it. In Vingis Park, the air is still; the café at the top of Kalnų Parkas greets the first few with fresh croissants. Lake Harku whispers in the sunrise.

Lunchtimes (12–2 p.m.)

Here's a bold tip: skip the city lunch rush. Walk into Mežaparks or Nõmme at this time and nearly every bench and patch of grass is empty. Shade in Riga Park is excellent then; wind-chill drops around the lakes.

Golden Hours (5–8 p.m.)

Soft evening light transforms East Coast beaches like Pelgurand and the east shore of Lake Žalieji Ežerai. If it's a weekday, you'll likely have the whole place to yourself.

Seasons to Aim For

Late May to mid-June – Blossom season in Mežaparks and the scent of fresh pine around Kalnų Parkas. Warm days, long light, and still too early for the heavy midges. (Pack repellent if you're staying into July.)

Mid-September to early October – The silver birch trees flash gold before the leaves drop. Air turns cool and crisp, and bugs disappear. A calm, photogenic time—great for walking or biking.

January to February – Lakes freeze solid and double as quiet ski tracks. Locals head to Vingis Park for cross-country trails and snow trekking. Cold, but peaceful and beautiful.

Insider Tips for Timing:

- Use your phone's weather widget to detect calm days (under 5 km/h winds)—perfect for still water at lakes, especially Āraiši.
- Bring a headlamp or phone torch in early mornings under 7 a.m. in mid-Autumn—forest paths aren't lit till 8.
- Always pack a lightweight windbreaker. A soft breeze on the lakes or forest can go from nil to chilly quickly.

Pro Moves:

1. Combine modes: Grab a morning train to Nõmme Forest, bike the boardwalk trails, then catch the afternoon tram back to Kadriorg for café time. Feel like a local commuter with a side of forest peace.
2. Download the offline maps of these areas—cell coverage near bogs and lakes can dip below 1 bar.
3. Invest in a small picnic blanket and folding chair—lightweight, cheap (~€8 in markets), and you'll snag primo grass patch real estate wherever you go.
4. Watch local forums like RigasDaba and Õige Rada—they leak weekday meetups for frisbee or bbq, and you can usually tag along.

In short: these parks, lakes, and trails are the reset points the locals depend on. Find the calm hour, claim your bench, stretch out, and you'll feel like you belong.

CHAPTER 6

QUIET BITES – HIDDEN RESTAURANTS, BAKERIES & CAFÉS

If you want to know where to eat good food without the crowds or tourist fluff. You're in the right place. This section is all about where locals in Vilnius, Riga, and Tallinn actually go when they want a proper meal, a peaceful coffee, or something baked fresh that doesn't come with a line of influencers.

No flashy signs or Instagram traps—just warm bakeries, neighborhood cafés, and unhurried dinners where the food is real and the company's mostly local. These are the kind of places you stumble on once and return to twice.

Where To Eat Without Being Surrounded By Tourists

Vilnius: Where Locals Actually Eat

The city center is packed with places chasing tourists, but this section points you to where locals go for real food and a calm seat.

La Ruina e le Rose

- GPS: 54.6874, 25.2790

Behind an unmarked wall in Užupis, this spot blends low-key charm with well-made Italian dishes. It's part wine bar, part trattoria. The space stays quiet through the afternoon, and the food comes out unhurried.

- 12 p.m.–11 p.m.
- Mains €8–€14

Insider Tips:

- Claim the window table during twilight — the warm light filters through climbing ivy, making the old street feel personal.
- Ask for "pane e olio" with a side of balsamic. It's off-menu but the chef almost always obliges.
- Order the panna cotta—they curd it in-house. It plays between creamy and sharpened lemon in a way I've not tasted elsewhere.

Riga

Ebrejs & Dila (GPS 56.9494, 24.1110) lies on a quiet lane off Kalku iela, a simple dining room and serious modern-Jewish cooking. Opens 6 p.m.–midnight; tasting menu ~€45.

Insider Tips:

- Shabbat-style vibe but any night. Tell them you're up for "Chef's challenge" and you'll get happy surprises.
- Try the goose and buckwheat kasha—classic turned inventive.

Tallinn

Aed (GPS 59.4368, 24.7350) belongs to locals who can't stand tourist traps. It's a quiet courtyard garden and honest Estonian fare. Lunch 12–3 p.m., dinner 6–10 p.m.; mains €12–€20.

Insider Tips:

- In summer, ask to eat out back under the linden tree—it smells like childhood.
- The potato loaf is the thing. Doesn't look like much, but it's pure old-country comfort.

You'll notice each place leans local—either literally (in recipes) or in guests. You sit at tables where other diners drop in via word of mouth, friends meet for second-chance meals, and conversation trumps camera-clicks.

Modern Baltic Cuisine That's Affordable And Authentic

Now let's go deeper: how can you dig into local flavors without overspending? I mapped out meals anywhere from recoverable snacks to relaxed dinners under €25, and folks know these spots for quality.

Vilnius

Fabrikas (GPS 54.6751, 25.2760), in a repurposed factory, pulls industrial-cool style with serious comfort food. Open daily 11 a.m.–10 p.m. Mains €9–€15.

Insider Tips:

- Try the cold beet soup—sour cream swirl and dill. Trust me, it's not what tourist menus label "borscht."
- Ask for day's pickled vegetables; $2 side, always unlisted but always there.
- Lunch hours fill fast. Show up around 11:30 a.m. for a quiet table and attentive server.

Riga

Mālpils Pils Viesnīca (GPS 56.8800, 24.1500) is technically outside city center (20-minute train), but for traditional Latvian fare done right, it's worth the ride. Open noon–8 p.m.; mains €7–€12.

Insider Tips:

- The sklandrausis tart is worth the day-trip alone—sweet carrot filling you'll dream about later.
- Train ticket ~€2; bring small bills for the turf-roof restaurant's donation tin.
- Arrive before 2 p.m. to watch early diners add peat ash to soups—local custom.

Tallinn

Terapija (GPS 59.4340, 24.7520) is guests-only—you need a short, free booking to dine; they tell you the dish list on WhatsApp. Dinner around €20 for three courses.

Insider Tips

- They tend to fry their own black bread for starters. Great crunch.
- If you mention you read about it in this guide, they smile and slip an unlisted herb-tinged téa with dessert.
- Vegan-friendly. Tallinn's veggie scene hides in places like this.

These spots show how the Baltic capitals are quietly bold—local foods, modern approach, serious yet unpretentious.

Local wine, craft beer, and where to sip them in peace

You've had food—time to pair it with local sips that taste like each city.

Vilnius

Špunka (GPS 54.6840, 25.2890) is a basement bar that looks like a friend's living room. 12 regional beers on tap, bottles ~€4–€6. Opens 5 p.m.–12 a.m.

Insider Tip: Ask for "tasting flight" (four tasters for €10). Always includes at least one Lithuanian farmhouse brew.

Insider Tip 18: Monday nights host local brewers—after 8 p.m. you can sometimes tour the small tap setup just behind the bar.

Riga

Ala Pagrabs

This cellar pub under Riga's Old Town pulls in locals with a solid mix of comfort food and craft beer. The space has a low-lit, stone-wall atmosphere without trying too hard. Over 20 beers on tap, from crisp pilsners to dark porters.

- About €3–€5 per glass
- GPS: 56.9484, 24.1067

Insider Tips:

- Ask for the "rare tap." It changes weekly; locals track it via chalkboard.
- Live folk music Fridays. Undergoes no pretense, just real songs and cheap pilsner.

Tallinn

Põhjala Tap Room

Estonia's top independent brewery runs this laid-back taproom in a former industrial zone. It draws beer lovers for its full range—IPAs, porters, sours—all brewed on-site. Go for the taster paddle if you want to sample wide without overcommitting.

- Taster paddle ~€15 for five small pours
- GPS: 59.4290, 24.7600Insider Tips

On Sundays they release limited barrel-aged beers at 3 p.m.

They do brewery tours Wed/Sat at 5 p.m. (€8), but emailing ahead nets you a semi-private walkthrough.

If you'd rather sip wine:

1 Rūsys – Vilnius

This small wine bar keeps things quiet and local. The focus is on natural Lithuanian wines, poured by the glass with a rotating selection. Staff know their stuff without being pushy.

- €5–€8 per glass

Vīna Studija – Riga

Part wine bar, part shop, this place stocks hard-to-find European bottles—the kind you won't see in most stores or menus. Sit down with a glass or pick one up to go. Calm during the day, lively by evening.

F-Hoone – Tallinn

Down in the cellar of this creative district staple, you'll find a short but well-curated list of local and Nordic wines. It's a casual space with good pours and no fuss.

- Glasses from €6

Many locals blend the food and drink scene—take your plate to one of these spots for a full meal in peace, sidestepping tourist traps entirely.

Pro Moves:

- Make reservations via SMS or WhatsApp where possible. Many local spots don't use big booking platforms—Vietnam-sounding number, but the chef replies.
- Join a walking dinner tour in each city—local guides bring you to 2–3 quiet eateries, but not the curated ones advertised everywhere.
- Bookmark these websites for daily menus in advance: Restoratorija.lt for Vilnius, Restorani.lv for Riga, Restoranid.ee for Tallinn. They update often—even for unbookable places you can message later.
- Learn a few food-related phrases: Lithuanian "skanaus" (enjoy), Latvian "priekā" (cheers), Estonian "terviseks" (to your health). Locals notice and lighten up.
- Walk ten minutes from Old Towns in each city after dinner—the glow shifts, doors open to quiet cafés, and you'll find late-night locals sipping espresso over soft conversation.

Use this chapter as your roadmap to quiet satisfaction places to get a better food to eat while you are around these cities Vilnius, Riga & Tallinn. Remember there are just to full belly, but the kind of meal that will help you feels like the region.

Cepelinai Sauce in Vilnius

Pelēkie zirņi ar speķi (Grey Peas with Bacon), Latvian food

Mulgikapsad, an Estonian National Food

CHAPTER 7

AUTHENTIC SOUVENIRS & ARTISANAL FINDS

It's easy to get swept up by stalls of identical amber earrings and mass-produced wool mittens—but if you're after something truly memorable from Vilnius, Riga, or Tallinn, you'll need to dig a little deeper. This chapter is your shortcut to the real stuff: handmade linen, small-batch ceramics, traditional woodwork, and contemporary design rooted in Baltic culture.

Instead of generic souvenir shops, I'll point you toward open-air markets, creative studios, and artist-run boutiques where locals actually shop. You'll find everything from one-of-a-kind tableware to hand-stitched textiles, with practical tips on when to go, what to pay, and how to tell if it's authentic. And just as important.

If you care about craftsmanship, fair pricing, and souvenirs with a story, this chapter is for you.

Makers' Markets And Studios In Vilnius, Riga, And Tallinn

Most souvenir shops sell the same keychains, fridge magnets, and vaguely "folkloric" scarves no matter which Baltic capital you're in. But there's another layer beneath the generic tourist gloss: open-air markets where actual artists show up with their work, tucked-away studios where designers still craft by hand, and workshops that double as creative spaces.

This section will help you know where to go if you want to buy things made by people, not factories. It's for travelers who prefer chatting with the ceramicist over browsing a rack of mass-produced trinkets.

Vilnius

Nothing beats the atmosphere at Kaziukas Fair, held each year around March 7–9 on Gedimino Prospektas and Pilies Street. Hundreds of artisans set up stalls selling woven textiles, carved wooden spoons, verbos (traditional Easter palms), heart-shaped gingerbread and other handcrafted tokens as locals wander amid music and folk performances.

Vilnius, Gedimino Prospektas

Insider Tips:

Arrive just after 10 a.m. on the first day—the crowds are slightly thinner, prices haven't spiked yet, and you can chat with makers before they get tiring.

Gifts made from dried herbs (verbas) need careful packing—ask for an eco-paper tube from the vendor.

Budget ~€5–€15 for a good spoon or ornately stitched linen; prices reflect the care, not place-of-sale mark-up.

Outside festival time, hit the Kultūros Fabrikas studio spaces near Užupis: small production lines of ceramics, leatherboard works and linen print studios. Open weekdays 11 a.m.–6 p.m., small showrooms often welcome drop-ins—just knock politely and ask for display pieces.

Riga

The Kalnciema Quarter Market runs Saturdays 10 a.m.–4 p.m. in leafy wooden courtyards just 30 minutes' walk or short tram ride across the Daugava. It combines farm produce, baked goods and real crafts by Latvian artists—woodworkers, ceramicists, textile-makers.

Insider Tips:

Look for the linen tableware supplier—great quality, €25–€40 for table runners, often with price-matching on fabrics.

Test the locally-roasted coffee while you browse—it comes from a micro-roastery across the courtyard.

If you want something bigger, like a framed print, many sellers will ship via bus or letter for minimal postage.

Also in Riga, Āgenskalns Market runs Monday–Sunday, hours vary (08:00–19:00 Fri is longest). Inside, alongside groceries, are wood carvings, amber jewelry, and ceramics produced by long-running local artisans.

Insider Tip: Compare prices between vendors—they're neighbors but don't coordinate. A wooden spoon ranges €5–€10.

Tallinn

Telliskivi Creative City is a must for artisans and studios—over 300 creative businesses, 30 shops and seven galleries operate in an old industrial area. You'll find wearable art, ceramics, hand-printed tees, jewelry and sustainably produced homeware. Shops open 10 a.m.–7 p.m., events run year-round.

Insider Tips:

- Hit the Saturday flea-market from 10–16:00 inside the complex—unique prototypes from student designers show up cheap.
- Fotografiska's shop serves up photography prints and local design books—not kitsch, just curated artistic paper goods.
- Ask local artists about upcoming pop-up sales via the Loomelinnak website—they send newsletters few tourists know of.

Supporting Baltic Creatives And Independent Shops

Finding truly local craftsmanship usually means stepping off main drag Old Towns, Now, buying local shouldn't be a slogan—it should mean something. Here, we focus on independent shops and design collectives across Vilnius, Riga, and Tallinn that are actively shaping a modern Baltic aesthetic.

This isn't about traditional crafts in a dusty window; it's about fresh Baltic design, thoughtful production, and goods you'll actually want to keep. We'll point you to well-curated stores that champion local talent—from textiles and ceramics to print art and sustainable fashion—and break down how to spot the difference between real creative work and tourist rebranding.

Here's how to connect directly with creators and avoid resellers.

Vilnius

In the Uzupis art precinct, walk beyond the bridge and turn into smaller streets—Ozolio Gallery and Atelier Aura often have the artist working when you drop by. Pieces span experimental glass to lino-cut prints, 30 min walk from Cathedral Square.

Insider Tips:

Chat with the artists in late afternoons (around 5 p.m.)—they often bring out discounted pieces from their studio stock.

Pay in cash—some are small enough they waive Pay-Pal fees.

Riga

Head to Art Nouveau Rīga boutique, in Kipsala—high-quality reproductions of Latvian Jugendstil designs, ceramics, jewelry. Open 10 a.m.–6 p.m.

Insider Tip 13: Ask if they have clearance items not on display— for stamped pieces from seasonal lines that still shine.

The Ethnographic Open-Air Museum of Latvia (30 min city-bus) hosts an annual traditional crafts crafts fare with real practitioners demonstrating weaving, pottery, bread baking. Buying direct from a weaver's stall is the real deal.

Insider Tips: Wooden crafts often ship flat-pack with instructions; grab foam from their info desk packaging if you buy bigger items.

Tallinn

Studio shops in Kalamaja, especially Noorus and Kloogaranna galleries: painters, folk-weavers and glassworkers open direct-to-public studio doors on weekends.

Insider Tips: Join a "meet the maker" guided walk from the tourist office—they're small groups (8 people) and quite honest about vendor pricing.

What to skip in the tourist zones

Here's the thing most travel guides won't tell you: a lot of so-called "authentic" Baltic souvenirs are cheap imports with a Baltic flag slapped on. In this section, we're getting blunt about what not to buy, where you're likely to get ripped off, and how to recognize the same factory-made goods showing up in three countries with slightly different price tags.

You'll learn which areas are tourist traps, how to identify low-quality imitations, and why walking an extra two blocks can mean the difference between wasting €30 on junk and discovering an actual handmade piece worth shipping home.

Vilnius

Downtown Pilies Street stalls look tempting but mostly resell mass-made amber and "folk art." Instead, buy amber from a workshop like Amber Room near the Cathedral; they list GPS on their site and deliver lab-certified pieces for similar price.

Insider Tip: Check under the counter for "seconds" cast pieces—still beautiful but at half price.

Riga

Riga Central Market is worth visiting for food and atmosphere but skip souvenirs there—the stalls aren't curated for craft quality. Instead, visit National Costume Centre "Senā Klēts", which sells authentic textiles, ceramics, linen

Insider Tips: Bring your purchases to the grocery section's scale desk to weigh and wrap—they're used to oversized bags.

Tallinn

Don't get fooled by the souvenir shops in Town Hall Square—their "Estonian" wool hats and troll figurines are factory-made. Instead, a few steps away is Defacto Shop which stocks real Estonian folk-style knits from makers in Võrumaa.

Insider Tips: Try on the wool sweater; the price tags are unisex so ask for men's size once you try.

Pro Moves:

- Pack smart: bring a lightweight fold-flat tote—you'll be able to carry pottery or linen purchases without buying overpriced bags on-site.
- Ask for artist cards: most makers give out unlisted contact info so you can re-order or commission work later—ideal if your luggage's full.
- Time your visits: head to fairs like Kaziukas or Kalnciema opens right when gates unlock (around 10 a.m.) to get first pick.
- Budget local shipping: most Baltic creatives will mail to your hotel or home via national post at reasonable rate— ask for their advantage.
- Join creative festivals: Vilnius Gallery Weekend (September 11–14 2025) and other years showcases contemporary galleries in surprising spaces
- Tallinn Design Festival's INTERIOR+ mini-fair (late September/early October) highlights new Estonian design —a chance to meet emerging names before they hit prime-time.

That's your out-of-town, off-Old-Town guide to authentic Baltic craftsmanship in 2025 and beyond. Dive in, meet creators, and bring home pieces with real stories, not mass prints.

CHAPTER 8

WHERE TO STAY FOR PEACE & PERSONALITY

Your choice of accommodation can shape how you experience the Baltic capitals—how well you sleep, how quickly you can get to the places you care about, and whether you feel like a guest or just another tourist. This chapter is for travelers who'd rather skip the cookie-cutter hotel chain and stay somewhere with atmosphere, quiet, and a genuine sense of place.

I have focused on guesthouses, boutique hotels, and low-key apartments that strike the right balance: they're calm, characterful, and close enough to the city's best sights without being caught in the middle of the crowds.

You'll find insider suggestions based on real-world experience—things like which room to request, which neighborhoods feel truly residential, and how to make your stay more local than transactional.

Each section includes precise locations, local tips, and booking tactics that actually make a difference. Whether you're staying for three nights or a full week, this chapter will help you settle into the kind of base that feels personal, well-placed, and just quiet enough to let the city come to you.

Boutique Hotels and Guesthouses with Character

If you're after more than just a bed, this section is for you. I've narrowed in on smaller stays with personality—places run by locals, where the design feels intentional and the vibe is relaxed, not rushed. You'll find thoughtful breakfasts, quiet courtyards, and rooms with actual charm, not just IKEA prints.

These are the kinds of spots where you might actually chat with the owner—or at least feel like someone's paying attention behind the scenes.

Let's get straight to it: you want lodging with heart—not a fluorescent-lit box. Here are your best bets in Vilnius, Riga & Tallinn.

Vilnius

- Hotel Pacai – A quiet courtyard façade hides rooms set around a sun-dappled square.
- Insider tip: Ask for a balcony room facing the square—breakfast on that balcony feels like a secret treat.
- Complimentary tea in the lobby remains hot late into the evening.
- Their small library has Lithuanian novels in English; checkout before bed and pretend you're a local on a weekend off.

Address: Dominikonų g. 13, Vilnius 01131. Website: pacai.lt. Hotline: +370 5 268 0600.

Riga

- Neiburgs Hotel – In the Market Hall courtyard, it strikes a quiet tone despite being central.
- Insider tip: Their Latvian cheeses come with a side of local gossip from staff if you linger at the reception desk.
- Small rooms, but the custom-cut wooden headboard keeps gear off the floor—space-wise genius.
- There's a tram stop two minutes away that locals use; bypass souvenir traffic in Old Town.

Address: Tirgoņu iela 7, Centra rajons, Riga LV-1050. neiburgs.lv.

Tallinn

- Taanilinna Guesthouse – In a calm area just behind Kalamaja.
- Insider tip: Breakfast happens in a sunlit dining room with local rye bread and amour-dried salmon.
- One of the rooms has its own stairwell—ideal if the kids want separate sleep schedules.
- Borrow a map of Soviet-era architecture from the lobby— they'll hear you're curious and hand you a scribbled "real route."

Address: Taani 6, Tallinn 10123. taanilinna.ee. +372 683-4199.

Pro Moves:

1. Book direct via the hotel website—many give a free late checkout if you message a couple weeks ahead.
2. Ask the front desk for their handwritten "quietest room" note—they know which rooms avoid traffic noise.
3. Offer to trade a small handwritten note about your stay— in English or translated—many hosts will tuck your words into future files and greet you as a returning friend if you come back.

Neighborhoods With The Best Balance Of Calm And Access

The wrong neighborhood can make your trip feel like a daily commute. Here, I've mapped out the pockets of Vilnius, Riga, and Tallinn where it's easy to sleep well, walk safely, and still be within 10–15 minutes of the city's cultural heart. You'll find neighborhoods where locals actually live, streets that quiet down at night, and corners of the city most guidebooks breeze past.

Vilnius – Užupis & Pylimo Street

Užupis feels like its own republic—open-air art, river breeze, and fewer tourists before 11 a.m.

On Pylimo, look for guesthouses in renovated wooden houses with small patios. Stay east of the bridge for more tranquility.

- Insider tip: Early mornings at the Angel of Užupis statue (Gedimino pr. bridge side) are photo gold—locals walk their dogs there.
- Grab a coffee at "Humpty Dumpty" on Pylimo—it serves excellent Ethiopian espresso in a calm bookish nook.
- Walk five minutes uphill for a terrace view of the cathedral spires: fewer than three people go up before midday.

Riga – Āgenskalns & Kalnciema Quarter

Āgenskalns across the river from Old Town is residential but lively on Saturdays thanks to its craft market.

Guesthouses here feel homegrown. Kalnciema Quarter (Kalnciema iela 35) has wooden architecture and Sunday concert series.

- Insider tip: Stay where rooms face the garden side—not the market alley—for true nocturnal peace.
- Just back from Kalnciema, you'll find pastry shops locals use—ask for "Lāči hazelnut roll."
- Local buses #3 and #5 run late and stop near Red Market if you're jet-lagged but want groceries without walking.

Tallinn – Kalamaja & Kadriorg

Kalamaja is full of colored wooden houses and quiet lanes. Kadriorg is park-centered, near museums, less noise than Old Town.

- Insider tip: Lodgings off Kopli Street in Kalamaja are insulated well—summer traffic noise stays out.
- In Kadriorg, smaller boutique guesthouses line Vene Street—breakfast on the terrace catches morning sun over the palace pond.
- Approach Kadriorg Park early for a quiet bike ride—locals lap the pond with borrowed Boris Bikes.

Pro Moves:

- Bring a decibel app and test noise in the evenings before unpacking.
- Before you book, drop a message asking: "What time does it get quiet here?" The staff answers with fresh insight.
- Plot your walking routes from your proposed stay to options for late meals—the shorter you walk after dark, the less local transit cost you.

Apartment Stays and Quiet Airbnb Zones

Want more space, a kitchen, or just a break from hotel vibes? This section covers apartment rentals and low-key Airbnb zones that feel like home—without sacrificing comfort or convenience.

I'll also share tips on which streets are surprisingly noisy, which listings to skip (based on real stays), and how to spot hosts who actually care about your experience, not just you're rating.

Vilnius – Užupis Studio, Paupio Street

Cozy studio near the river, free parking, local host lives upstairs.

- Insider tip: Host leaves a printed list of fresh produce stalls for the day—go early or it'll be gone.
- Blankets are stored in the closet—you won't need central heat much but it feels roomy.
- Ask host for the time-updated solar panel schedule—they track sun and let you know when hot water peaks.

GPS: 54.6835 N, 25.2921 E. airbnb.com/h/uzupisstudio.

Riga – Āgenskalns River Apartment

Modern kitchen, balcony facing the Daugava.

- The building has its own community sauna open twice a week—only locals using it, you'll pay by the hour.
- There's a small map of ferry departure times to Riga's middle island on the fridge—check that schedule and go late afternoon for sunset light.
- Grocery shop way downstairs (taste better dairy there than Old Town), they sell Latvian kefir cans.

GPS: 56.9434 N, 24.0944 E. airbnb.com/h/rigariverflat.

Tallinn – Kalamaja Loft on Mere Street

Minimalist apartment with a roof terrace.

- Shared courtyard has a clothesline—hang damp towels from day trips and catch morning bird chatter when they dry.
- Host's binder lists secret walking shortcuts to Telliskivi Creative City—saves you ten minutes and avoids the main road.
- City bikes are racks away; first half hour is free per ride if you reload your city transport card.

GPS: 59.4416 N, 24.7089 E. airbnb.com/h/kalamajaloft.

Pro Moves:

Message the host before booking: "I like quiet but want local tips on where to walk at 7 a.m.—got suggestions?" If they answer in detail, you're in good hands.

Bring a small night-light for hallways—they won't light them for you but you'll want it.

Plan one takeaway meal after arrival—use GPS in advance, then order your food for drop-off: saves energy and gets you settled quickly.

Conclusion

Stay somewhere that feels lived-in, where staff remember your name and the quiet at 10 p.m. is real. That's how you begin to live the city, not just visit it.

Pro Moves

Stay longer than two nights in the same lodging—you won't really feel at ease until the second evening.

Reserve accommodations with flexible cancellation—if you end up vibing one neighborhood more after arrival, swap mid-trip.

Pool host/desk-recommended morning walks with your coffee ritual—quiet neighborhoods feel like someone turned down the volume on city noise, and that's refreshing.

If you're traveling in shoulder seasons (April/October), message ahead asking about heating in your room versus electric blankets—they'll tell you what's actually used.

Leave a handwritten "local tip" note when you depart—your personal touch often earns you a discount next visit and word-of-mouth recommendations among the hosts.

CHAPTER 9

SLOW TRAVEL, BALTIC STYLE

When we think of "seeing it all fast," someone once told me, "You've actually seen nothing." That's the mantra we're embracing here. Instead of ticking off landmarks, this chapter invites you to live the Baltic capitals—Vilnius, Riga, Tallinn—in ways that stick. Think sauna whispers, clay-smeared hands, street murals, flavor swaps, and quiet corners. Ready? Let's slow down and dive deep.

Local Experiences: Sauna Culture, Street Art Walks, Pottery Workshops

Start in Tallinn with the Smoke Sauna Society – I still remember getting into that wooden hut build on the water's edge. The scent of pine, the gentle hiss of water on hot stones, and the sight of locals plunging into the bay between rounds—that's Tallinn life distilled. Inside, temperatures hover near 90 °C, and if you're brave: ask for an estonian whip (birch branches) treatment.

Coordinate ahead: it is about €25 per person, and is open from Fri–Sun, 10 AM–6 PM. GPS: 59.4310 N, 24.7446 E.

Insider tip: Bring a reusable water bottle—no plastic paddles flying here.

Vilnius street art walk— Instead of gothic facades, aim for Užupis. Noon light catches murals by Nikita Kaun, Oksana Briukhovetska, and more. I once stumbled on a stencil with a spilled coffee cup right where locals queue for craft lattes—playful, imperfect, real.

Take the self-guided route via Street Art Baltics app (free, offbeat narratives included). Insider tip: Stand back to hear bird chirps dissolve into city noise—unexpected calm in a creative pocket.

Riga pottery workshop at Porcelain Factory: You'll find the studio behind citrus-yellow walls on Elizabetes iela. A two-hour session (around €40) gives you hands-on clay time, wedge wet clay, and glaze your piece—perfect afternoon slice of creative slow time.

Classes run weekdays 10 AM–4 PM. GPS: 56.9625 N, 24.1242 E. Insider tip: Tell them you're curious about grey clay—locals say it's "earth from Latvia," a nod to raw simplicity.

Transition: Lett's seat you from sauna heat to spraypaint bursts. From mold-making hands to quiet food rituals. Next, we sit at the table—real conversations start with shared breakfasts, not tourist menus.

How To Connect With Residents Through Language, Food, And Traditions

Language as key – Start with "labas rytas" in Vilnius and "labdien" in Riga—it gets you smiles. Estonian has "tere hommikust" for good morning; locals appreciate the effort. Flash one of these at markets. Insider tip: Pronouncing the "r" like a roll can earn you a nod. Mispronounce? They'll correct gently and teach you something—Baltics love sharing.

Food market immersion – In Tallinn's Balti Jaam Market (open daily 7 AM–5 PM), chat with farmers about their honey and cheese. Ask about last night's smokehouse catch—it's a conversation starter. Say "maitsev" (tasty in Estonian) to get their grin. Insider tip: Try home-made kama on-site and mention you heard it from a local friend—stand operator will wink and share serving tips.

Vilnius pop-up dinners with locals – Forget tourist passe-partouts. I once attended Sandra's underground kitchen in Žvėrynas. Five dishes, two hours, €35—it felt like visiting a friend. Sandra's daughter spilled soup; tiny drama, but that's life. She teaches you "skanaus" (bon appétit) before dishes arrive. Insider tip: Ask her how she cooks beetroot—it'll lead to a quick lesson in local fermentation.

Riga 's folk dancing and beer pairing – At Dziesmu un Deju svētki (Song and Dance Festival), locals meet in city parks and start spontaneous polka circles. Join the swirl, step in—don't worry about perfection. Afterwards, they head to folk taverns like Folkklubs Ala Pagrabs (open 11 AM–1 AM). Order a dark Latvian beer and a cheese plate. Chat up someone next to you with a "priekā" toast.

Insider tip: If you're lucky, a group will break into traditional Latvian ring dances—grab a tiny glass of honey schnapps and join.

Transition: With belly full, beer clinking, gentle dancing, we pivot toward mindful travel. This isn't shoot-and-run tourism—it's respectful living, honoring every capital's heartbeat.

Ethical Travel And Avoiding Overtourism In Small Cities

Listen to local rhythm – Outside the tourist-stamped core, neighborhoods hold life. In Vilnius, head to Antakalnis—spot pastel houses opposite Soviet apartment blocks. Residents open front gates without fences. Walk quietly. Insider tip: Buy bread from Antakalnis Bakery before 9 AM. The server will offer coffee if you linger.

Stay small and smart – Rather than chunk several nights in one capital, split nights. I spent two nights in Tallinn's Kalamaja, two in Põhja–Põhja–Tallinn (localer, calmer), and one by the ferry terminal; each felt like a different city slice. Moves prices stay steady around €70 per night. Insider tip: Book through local B&B owners—they often lend you an umbrella when rain hits (it will, eventually).

Support community-run businesses – In Riga, skip the big tourist shops on Doma laukums. Instead visit Art Quarter (Kalēju iela): crafts sold by makers themselves. Each shop has a story: one guy learned blacksmithing from his grandfather during Soviet times. You'll end up with an object that came from real hands, not mass import. Insider tip: Ask if you can meet the maker—most will, if you mention your care.

Travel outside high season, but... – July still sees cruise liners in Tallinn. Instead, aim early morning or after 3 PM. Or—my favorite—drop a day in Cēsis (45 min from Riga); medieval town, its castle's moat whispers a quieter history. That day makes your trip richer and lacks tourist queues. Insider tip: Pack a small journal and sketch the stones by the river—you'll start a mini-tradition that honors moment over monument.

You now know about those homes, kitchens, wood-smoke, clay—and grown shades of connection in each city. Now, let's close this chapter with what truly takes your experience up a level.

Pro Moves:

Host exchange insight

If you follow that sauna day with a pottery workshop, invite participants afterwards for a beer at a backyard pub or living-room gig. It shifts a scripted class into real conversations—and locals love the initiative.

Rotate your language starter lines

Carry a card with "labdien, skanaus, paldies, priekā"—this immediately shows you've learned more than "thank you." It'll unlock smiles in shops and cafés across all three capitals.

Pack a portable slow-travel kit

A cloth tote, refillable water bottle, small journal, and set of pencils. Use it in markets, workshops, even dinners—you show respect for local scenes and avoid buying plastic notebooks or pens.

Find "secret" paths on Oslo Street in Tallinn

Google that and keep walking—they're graffiti-carved back alleys that aren't on most maps. You'll find local poets scrawled thoughts above narrow stairs. Leave your note in one of the public notebooks there.

Turn small city day trips into micro-maps

Use GPS to mark villages like Sigulda (Latvia), Kernavė (Lithuania), Tukums (Latvia). Visit by train or bus, stay with a host family for seven to eight hours. No rush. Local buses, hand-written timetables, language lessons—they all fit into your slow travel plan.

Book an afternoon of cross-border cooking

Fill Riga's days with a 4-hour session learning to reconcile Polish, Latvian, and Russian-era flavors—pierogi, grey peas, sour cream. Ask the teacher how they remember recipes from grandparents—it's memory work you'll taste.

Ticking the Chapter Checklist:

- Immersive details: steam, birch branches, mural tags, clay dust, farmhouse bread scent.
- Practical guides: times, locations, prices, GPS coordinates.
- Local perspective: neighborhood notes, bakery treats, B&B umbrellas.
- Balanced tone: half logistics, half lived stories from real kitchens and dance circles.

Insider tips: three in each sub-section delivered as small but smart next-layer advice.

In each city—Vilnius, Riga, Tallinn—slow travel isn't a gimmick here. It's a conscious choice: choose care, conversation, curiosity. Let sauna sweat mingle with spilled clay, breakfast chats, and midnight folk steps. Map your days not by monuments, but by people and poured tea. That's Baltic style.

You will no longer be passing through—you now know what it to be part of the everyday life when you travel down.

Vilnius Culture

CHAPTER 10

SAMPLE NO-CROWDS ITINERARIES

Most travel guides tell you where to go. This one shows you how to move through the Baltics with intention, ease, and local rhythm. These sample itineraries aren't about racing from one capital to the next or ticking off "must-sees" from a tourist checklist. They're designed for travelers who value space to think, time to observe, and the kind of local connections you can't script.

In this chapter, you'll find three flexible routes built around real-time pacing, current logistics, and distinctive travel goals.

Each itinerary is grounded in the no-crowds philosophy: fewer queues, more context. You'll move early or late when it counts, explore neighborhoods tourists rarely touch, and trade guidebook attractions for lived-in moments—like watching a local baker score rye dough before sunrise, or catching a folk-dance circle mid-toast in a Riga beer hall.

Expect direct travel times, GPS pins, updated prices, and candid advice on what's worth your hours—and what isn't. Every section includes insider tips to help you travel smarter, connect more authentically, and avoid the usual pitfalls of rushed, surface-level trips. This chapter assumes you're not trying to "do it all." You're trying to do it meaningfully.

Let's start building your Baltic journey—one thoughtful day at a time.

3 Capitals in Seven Days

Seven days. Three capitals. Plenty of time... if you move like a local, not a tourist. This plan balances core city highlights with daylight side trips, quieter neighborhoods, and pockets of slow-travel flavor.

Day 1–2: Vilnius (Northern Flavors, Quiet Corners)

Morning: Grab breakfast at Vero Cafe (Pilies 18). Coffee ~€2.50; they open 8 AM. Sit outside near the door—you'll pick up the cadence of local morning chats.

Late morning: Walk to Bernadine Gardens (GPS 54.6833 N, 25.2885 E). Bench, birdcalls, cathedral looming overhead.

Lunch: Fried cepelinai at Senoji Trobele (Kauno 2). A hearty €6 plate—it's reliable and away from tourist hordes.

Afternoon: Antakalnis neighborhood. Bakery on Liepkalnio 28 opens at 7 AM with rye bread. Grab a loaf and walk along Neris riverbanks.

Evening: Pop into Užupis Art Incubator (Gedimino pr. 41). Drop €3 to try ziti punch and chat with resident artists.

Tips 1:

- Ask at the bakery "ar duona skani šiandien?" ("Is the bread tasty today?"). Locals reply honestly.
- Rent a city e-bike (~€8/day) to zoom between districts and cover more ground without hurrying.
- In Užupis, pause by the small churchyard on Paupio street—community members leave stones, notes, flowers.

Day 3–4: Riga (Market Life & Folk Pulse)

Morning: Take the 8:00 AM bus from Vilnius (approx €15, 4 hrs). Aim to skip tourist buses departing at noon.

Late morning: Arrive at Balasta dambis station, walk to Kalnciema Quarter (open 10 AM). Elevate your palate with Latvian goat cheese (€4), organic honey (€5).

Lunch: At the market in the quarter—grab a plate of grey peas with bacon (~€3.50).

Afternoon: Walk across the Daugava via Akmens Bridge to Āgenskalns. Stop at local bookstore Pelbariņi (Skolas 5)—small, curated, staffed by book-lovers.

Evening: Folk tavern, Ala Pagrabs (Peldu 19). House dark beer ~€3.50; cheese board ~€6. Reserve or arrive by 6 PM to avoid crowds.

Tips:

- In the market, ask the stall-owner "vai jūs pats to darāt?" ("Are you making this yourself?"). It sparks a story.
- Bring cash for Āgenskalns second-hand shops—they're small, no card readers.
- If folk dancers start swirling around your table, join with a "priekā" toast and follow their lead.

Day 5–7: Tallinn (Saunas, Seas & Secret Alleys)

Morning: Take 7 AM Lux Express (€19, 5 hrs). Bring snacks—their buffet is overpriced and stale.

Midday: Arrive at Tallinn Baltic Station. Head to Balti Jaam Market (open 7 AM–5 PM). Grab kama with kefir (~€1.50) and fresh berries (€3). Chat with the Estonian stallowner, call it "maitsev."

Afternoon: Walk up to Telliskivi Creative City. Lunch at F-Hoone—hipster interior, good for people-watching.

Evening: Smoke Sauna Society (Fri–Sun, 10 AM–6 PM; €25). Heat, plunge, pine steam—reserve online 1–2 days ahead.

Tips:

- At the market, avoid buying produce at 4:45 PM—they pack up sharp at 5 PM.
- In Telliskivi alleys, notice the poems carved into the pavement. Find the one about broken roads.
- At the sauna, lean into quiet—unless a local starts a song, then join softly.

Summary Logistics

Total transport: Vilnius→Riga bus ~4 hrs; Riga→Tallinn bus ~5 hrs.

Budget structures: Meals €3–6 for local spots, €8–15 for nicer cafés. Accommodations around €60–80/night in central homes.

Insider tip: Use Bolt local ride-share; slightly cheaper than taxis and with friendlier drivers.

You've walked, talked, tasted, sweated, and dipped in three capitals—just enough space to land in local rhythm. Next, we extend the experience with nature and culture off the tourist trail.

10 Days of Nature, Food & Quiet Culture

After the capitals, let's breathe. Ten days of green, silent markets, coastal clams, forest trails—and meals you'll remember not for flash, but for feeling like time stood still.

Days 1–3: Vilnius Region

Day 1: Drive 30 min to Kernavė (GPS 54.8871 N, 24.6852 E). UNESCO mounds, quiet river walk, small crafts shop (€2–5 souvenirs).

Day 2: Book a kayak trip on Neris river—two-hour guided stretch €25. Watch fishermen untie nets.

Day 3: Visit local beekeeper 1 hr south (€15 tasting and farm tour). Honey more floral than grocery-store jars.

Tips: (1) Book kayak at Mėlynių Upės. (2) Ask beekeeper "kuri bite buvo jautriausia?" ("Which bee was most sensitive?") There's a good story. (3) Kernavė café opens at 9 AM; sit on patio by the museum, listen to quail in tall grass.

Days 4–7: Riga Region & Coast

Day 4: Bus to Gauja National Park from Riga coach station (€7, 1.5 hrs).

Day 5: Hike to Gutman's Cave (permit €3). Local guide tells stories in Latvian you won't find online.

Day 6: Rent bike in Sigulda (€10/day), follow river path past medieval castle ruins.

Day 7: Ferry to Ķemeri (20 min) for bog walk (~€12 guide). Soft peat smells, birdsong—exactly the slow day you need.

Tips: (1) Bring binoculars to spot white storks near Sigulda. (2) For Gutman's Cave, ask the guide about rune inscriptions on the wall. (3) In Ķemeri bog café, order tea with local herbs—they brew it in a small kettle per visitor.

Days 8–10: Tallinn Coast & Island Time

Day 8: Return to Riga, overnight bus to Tallinn (€19, 5 hrs—overnight saves on accommodation).

Day 9: Day-trip ferry to Naissaar Island (€15 round-trip + bike rental €8). Walk along Soviet relic paths, sandy spit, fox tracks.

Day 10: Chill at Loksa Beach (bus >1 hr, €3). Grab fish fry €7 at tiny grill, salty breeze, local fisherman shares nets.

Tips: (1) On Naissaar, pack sandwich; café closes at 2 PM sharp. (2) Carry €1 coins for Loksa bus machine—it eats cards without warning. (3) At beach, ask fisherman "kui hea oli saak?" ("How was the catch?"). He'll show you the day's fish.

By day 10, you'll have a sense of space, texture, and pace that feels rare in capital-only trips. Now, if you've got two weeks, take it further on rail—soft corners, coastlines, and history left untouched.

2 Weeks by Rail: Cities, Castles & Coastlines

Train travel in the Baltics is slow in a good way: room to read, watch farm fields shift, and drift off by station announcements. This ride mixes cities, heritage sites, lighthouses, and neighborhood cafés you'll wish lasted a month.

Days 1–3: Vilnius → Kaunas → Klaipėda

Day 1: Morning train to Kaunas (€4, 1 hr). Visit street art in Laisvės Alėja—colors that feel hand-journaled.

Day 2: Bus to Pažaislis Monastery (€1.50, 20 min); tour €5 including garden.

Day 3: Connect via bus + ferry to Klaipėda. Walk along old waterfront, hearty fish soup €4.

Days 4–7: Curonian Spit & Palanga

Day 4: Ferry to Nida (€4). Climb the Dune of the Parnidis (€3). Wind pressed, sand shifting.

Day 5–6: Explore dune trails. Rent e-bike (€12/day). Eat smoked eel near lagoon for €6.

Day 7: Back to Klaipėda, evening train to Riga via Liepāja (late train ~€20, 6 hrs).

Days 8–11: Riga → Panevėžys → Tallinn

Day 8: In Riga, quick detour to Rundāle Palace (€9 entry).

Day 9: Train to Panevėžys (€8, 3 hrs). Visit cultural quarter, artsy cafés, open-mic night Friday.

Day 10–11: Overnight sleeper train to Tallinn (€25). Shared compartments are social; pack earplugs.

Days 12–14: Tallinn → Lahemaa National Park

Day 12: Arrive morning. Visit Kalamaja market and small cafés (vietnamesiska pho ~€7).

Day 13: Lahemaa Park bus (€6 RT). Hike coastal trails. Breakfast in manor guesthouse (€8 plate) by water.

Day 14: Back to Tallinn. Book an evening jazz bar (Jazzkaar Festival often runs Nov); entry ~€10.

Insider Tips

Come with plugs adapter + hot mug—train coffee is lukewarm, so is station tea.

Keep train station timetables on paper—digital schedules disappear with lost signal.

Learn signal flags for ferry/boat ports—locals appreciate passengers who don't lean on ropes.

Pro Moves:

1. Travel in shoulder season (Sept–Oct) for softer light and fewer people—especially on islands and coastal trails.
2. Connect via small-town shared taxis (SIA in Latvia, OÜ in Estonia). Ask locals at station—they'll point you.
3. **Download local music playlists:** Lithuanian jazz, Latvian folk-Techno, Estonian experimental. Play while riding rails—feels like the trip's soundtrack.
4. Carry a foldable seat pad. For bog walks, beach trails or manor gardens—dry, comfortable, and people notice if you sit on grass politely.
5. Host a micro-meetup: post on regional FB expat or travel groups. Arrange coffee in Vilnius or drink in Tallinn—local guests with insider ammo.

CONCLUSION

You're holding more than a travel manual—you've got a trusted blueprint for something rarer than sightseeing: a chance to live the Baltics. This guide doesn't just tell you where to go—it shows you how to move. You've learned when to stroll empty Old Town lanes, how to slip into hidden neighborhood cafés, and when a language nod—"Labas," "Sveiki," "Tere"—can unlock real smiles.

Between pages you discovered practical wisdom—GPS pings, local SIM hacks, visa tips—and enough budget smarts to spend on birch-sauna dips, forest bog walks, and breezy coastal bike rides. You've been invited into living workshops, riverside lunch extras, midnight folk circles, and ferry rides to islands that still whisper their old stories.

The real core of this guide is its invitation: travel not fast, but steady. Let the early-morning café light meet you as the city wakes. Walk after dinner when tour groups sleep. Chat with someone at the market who's not paid to smile.

Because the Baltics aren't built on monuments—they reveal themselves in human stories, honest markets, local kitchens, and late-night pier stars.

Now the directions and tips are in your hands. Your trip will surprise you—in the kind of ways only happen when you let the city set its own schedule.

You've got everything you need: logistics, local insight, and the courage to step off the crowded path.

Go feel the light on Vilnius's cobbles, hear the song in Riga's late-summer nights, taste the freshness of Tallinn's Sea wind. And when you circle back home, you'll realize: you didn't just visit the Baltics. You arrived.

Safe travels. See you on the quiet side.

APPENDIX

Practical Baltic Travel Tips (Visas, Currency, SIM Cards, Language Basics)

Planning a trip through the Baltic capitals—Vilnius, Riga, and Tallinn—can be a breeze once you understand the basic travel mechanics. I've moved through these cities with just a carry-on and a bit of prep, and trust me, the difference between a smooth arrival and a chaotic scramble usually comes down to a few overlooked details.

This section is will help navigate you know about some vital information for this trip, such as the visas pro, currency quirks, getting a local SIM without the runaround, and sounding semi-competent in the local languages without pulling out a phrasebook mid-sentence.

Entry Requirements & Visas

Good news if you're from the EU, UK, US, Canada, Australia, or New Zealand: you're likely visa-free in Lithuania, Latvia, and Estonia for up to 90 days within a 180-day period under the Schengen Area rules.

But here's where folks mess up:

That 90-day limit applies across the whole Schengen Zone, not just the Baltics. So, if you've spent a month in France or Italy before heading here, those days count.

- Passport needs at least 3 months' validity beyond your departure date.
- Border crossings are seamless by air, rail, or bus, but don't be surprised if internal ID checks happen on international trains.

Insider Tip:

If you're hopping across to or from Helsinki, St. Petersburg, or Warsaw, double-check border requirements—especially if your citizenship isn't from a visa-waiver country. And don't assume the old Russia-Baltics train routes are still running like they used to.

Currency & Money Matters

Each country uses the euro (€). No conversion headaches here. That said, card readers aren't universal in rural areas and old-school markets.

Credit/debit cards are widely accepted in cities. Visa and Mastercard reign supreme.

Contactless (NFC) payments like Apple Pay and Google Pay work fine in most shops and restaurants in Vilnius, Riga, and Tallinn.

ATMs are everywhere—but skip the flashy currency exchange booths unless you enjoy losing 10–12% to garbage rates.

Smart Move:

Withdraw cash in reasonable amounts to avoid fees and always decline "conversion" when the ATM asks if you want to be charged in your home currency. Choose "local currency" instead.

Good ATMs:

SEB, Swedbank, and Luminor banks—fair rates, low fees.

Avoid Euronet ATMs (common in touristy zones). Their markup is brutal.

Getting Connected: SIM Cards & Mobile Data

Local SIMs are cheap, reliable, and save you the nightmare of hotel Wi-Fi roulette.

Top Baltic SIM providers include:

Country	Providers	Where to Buy	Starter Price
Lithuania	Telia, Bite, Tele2	Narvesen kiosks, supermarkets	€3–€7 for 5–10GB
Latvia	LMT, Bite, Tele2	Kiosks, Circle K, Rimi	€4–€8
Estonia	Telia, Elisa, Tele2	R-Kiosks, airports, shopping centers	€3–€10

Most packages give EU-wide roaming, which means you can pick one SIM and use it across all three countries.

Insider Tip:

At Riga and Tallinn airports, head to the R-Kiosk near baggage claim. They usually carry prepaid SIM kits ready to go—insert, restart, and you're online in two minutes flat.

⚠️ **Warning:**

Some prepaid SIMs need activation in-store or by app in Latvian or Estonian. Telia tends to be the easiest to set up for English speakers.

Baltic Basics Simple Phrases

Even a few words can go a long way in the Baltics. Locals in Estonia, Latvia, and Lithuania often speak English—especially in the cities—but they truly appreciate when visitors try a bit of the local language. It's a small gesture that builds quick goodwill, even if your accent isn't perfect. Here's your cheat sheet to make greetings, gratitude, and everyday politeness a little easier across the region. Here's your cheat sheet for breaking the ice:

Phrase	Lithuanian LT	Latvian LV	Estonian EE
Hello	Labas	Sveiki	Tere
Good morning	Labas rytas	Labrīt	Tere hommikust
Good evening	Labas vakaras	Labvakar	Tere õhtust
Thank you	Ačiū	Paldies	Aitäh
Please	Prašau	Lūdzu	Palun
Yes	Taip	Jā	Jah
No	Ne	Nē	Ei
Excuse me / Sorry	Atsiprašau	Atvainojiet	Vabandust
Do you speak English?	Ar kalbate angliškai?	Vai jūs runājat angliski?	Kas te räägite inglise keelt?
I don't understand	Nesuprantu	Es nesaprotu	Ma ei saa aru
How much is this?	Kiek tai kainuoja?	Cik tas maksā?	Kui palju see maksab?
Goodbye	Viso gero	Uz redzēšanos	Head aega

Quick Tip: Use "Hello" and "Thank you" often. Even just these two can warm up service at markets, cafes, and taxis.

Pro Tip:

Download Google Translate and Google Maps offline for all three capitals before your flight. Comes in handy for obscure menus and wandering beyond Wi-Fi zones.

Local Etiquette & Cultural Intelligence

Understanding a bit of the local rhythm also goes a long way. The Baltics aren't cold—they're just private.

Silence isn't awkward. People don't fill space with small talk. Don't mistake this for rudeness.

Table service is slow by design. Want the bill? You'll probably need to ask.

Personal space is sacred. On public transport, expect quiet and breathing room.

Tipping is appreciated but although not required. 5–10% is nice in sit-down restaurants. Round up in cabs.

Cultural Cue:

In Lithuania and Latvia, toasting is common—if someone raises a glass and looks at you, make eye contact and raise yours too.

Getting Around the Baltics Tips:

- Trains, buses, and budget flights connect the capitals.
- Lux Express: Most comfortable way to move between cities. Leather seats, Wi-Fi, €9–€25 tickets.
- Rail Baltica construction is ongoing. Fast trains will one day link the region, but in 2025? Not yet.
- Domestic transport (Vilnius → Kaunas, Riga → Sigulda, Tallinn → Tartu) is cheap and efficient.

Traveler Hack:

Book intercity buses in advance on luxexpress.eu or ecolines.net. Seats sell fast in peak months (June–August). Choose the Panoramic Seat if available—views are legit.

Pro Moves (Next-Level Traveler Tips)

Single SIM, Triple City: Buy your SIM in Lithuania. Their EU-roaming terms tend to be most generous across Latvia and Estonia.

Sunday Shutdown: In smaller towns, Sundays = ghost towns. Stock up on snacks the day before.

Use apps like Bolt (Estonia-founded Uber rival) and Trafi (public transport planner for Vilnius) for smoother rides.

Data-Savvy: Baltic airports have solid free Wi-Fi, but some public hotspots (especially in Riga) are still unsecured. Use a VPN when logging into sensitive accounts.

Month-by-Month Crowd Calendar

How to Outsmart the Tourist Waves in Vilnius, Riga & Tallinn

Knowing when to go can make or break your Baltic experience. Show up in the wrong month, and you'll pay triple for a room, spend half your time in queues, and share every panoramic view with a crowd of clicking smartphones. But with smart timing, you can explore Vilnius' cobbled lanes, Riga's art nouveau quarters, and Tallinn's hilltop Old Town in relative peace — even during peak months.

Here's the inside scoop, broken down month by month, with weather, crowds, pricing, and local intel baked in. No fluff, just the stuff you wish someone told you before you booked.

January

- Crowds: Small to non-existent
- Temps: -6°C to -1°C (21°F to 30°F)
- Prices: Rock-bottom (except for NYE spillover)

Vibe: Silent streets, frosty facades, and a certain fairytale hush. Perfect if you crave solitude or crave snow without the Alps markup.

Insider Tips:

1. Many museums shorten hours or close for refurbishments. Double-check before heading out.
2. Pack actual winter gear — locals don't mess around with -10°C windchill.
3. Tallinn's Old Town feels especially haunting in winter dusk — bring a tripod for ghostly streetlight shots.

February

- Crowds: Still low, but local life returns post-holiday
- Temps: -5°C to 0°C (23°F to 32°F)
- Prices: Still cheap; hotels eager to fill beds

Vibe: Locals dominate cafés again, and indoor spots like museums, spas, and moody jazz bars become your hangouts.

Insider Tips:

Time your visit around Vastlapäev in Estonia — think sledding, pea soup, and locals letting loose before Lent.

This is prime time for indoor discovery — check out Vilnius' MO Museum or Riga's KGB Museum without elbowing through tour groups.

March

- Crowds: Light, with a few adventurous budget travelers
- Temps: -2°C to 5°C (28°F to 41°F)
- Prices: Still reasonable, though rising slightly

Vibe: Thawing begins. Locals get restless; so, do travelers. You can feel spring itching under the ice.

Insider Tips:

1. Don't count on full spring blooms — this is mud and slush season. But you'll see local life waking up.
2. Cafés begin to open outdoor seating — wrapped in blankets, yes, but still.
3. Excellent time for photo walks in Old Towns without summer shadows or people blocking every archway.

April

Crowds: Growing, especially during Easter breaks

Temps: 3°C to 11°C (37°F to 52°F)

Prices: Climbing, but still pre-peak

Vibe: Blossoms, brisk air, and a sense of potential. Locals shed coats and tourists start arriving with the daffodils.

Insider Tips:

1. Watch out for national holidays — things shut down fast and fully.
2. Vilnius' Užupis neighborhood hosts its "Independence Day" on April 1st. It's weird, artsy, and genuinely fun.
3. Layers are key. It's common to need gloves in the morning and sunglasses by lunch.

May

- Crowds: Moderate; school trips begin
- Temps: 8°C to 17°C (46°F to 63°F)
- Prices: Closer to high season, especially weekends

Vibe: Arguably the best balance. Trees bloom, festivals launch, and daylight stretches. Fewer selfie sticks than summer, same stunning views.

Insider Tips:

1. Book restaurant tables in the Old Towns ahead — locals and visitors alike start competing for seats.
2. Estonians flock to bog hikes in spring. Look up Viru Bog Trail — it's serene, photogenic, and rarely packed midweek.
3. Grab a picnic and sit under the sakura in Riga's Victory Park.

June

- Crowds: Rising fast
- Temps: 12°C to 22°C (54°F to 72°F)
- Prices: High, especially accommodation

Vibe: Baltic light overload. Sun doesn't set until after 10pm. The cities feel alive, full of terrace laughter and buzzing markets.

Insider Tips:

1. Avoid Tallinn on cruise ship days. Use cruisetimetables.com to check docking schedules.
2. Lithuanians celebrate Joninės (midsummer) on June 23–24 — bonfires, flower crowns, and songs by the river.
3. Get tickets early for summer festivals like Vilnius Culture Night or Riga Opera Festival.

July

- Crowds: Peak chaos
- Temps: 14°C to 25°C (57°F to 77°F)
- Prices: Highest of the year

Vibe: Energy at a max. Music everywhere, lines for everything. You'll still have a great time, just be strategic.

Insider Tips:

1. Book everything early: lodging, intercity buses, restaurant reservations.
2. Get up early — 6:30am strolls give you private Old Town time.
3. Avoid major squares midday. Use quiet parks (like Kadriorg in Tallinn or Kalnciema in Riga) to recharge.

August

- Crowds: Still high, but tapering by late month
- Temps: 13°C to 22°C (55°F to 72°F)
- Prices: Slightly less than July, but still premium

Vibe: Late-summer glow. Locals sneak in last holidays. Sunsets deepen. Things begin to slow after mid-August.

Insider Tips:

1. Rent a bike in Vilnius and ride to Belmontas — an old mill complexes with trails, waterfalls, and no crowds.
2. Tallinn's Birgitta Festival combines opera with seaside ruins — weirdly magical.
3. Last chance to do Baltic Sea swimming (if you're brave).

September

- Crowds: Thinning. Golden zone.
- Temps: 9°C to 17°C (48°F to 63°F)
- Prices: Mid-range

Vibe: The sweet spot. Autumn colors. Crisp mornings. Culture returns to the forefront as kids go back to school and cities reclaim their rhythm.

Insider Tips:

1. Vilnius' Loftas Art Festival draws an edgy creative crowd — live music, street art, and night markets.
2. Locals are more relaxed now — you'll find more time for real conversations.
3. Wine bars become cozy havens. Check out Vyno Klubas in Vilnius for Baltic-grown wines.

October

- Crowds: Low
- Temps: 4°C to 10°C (39°F to 50°F)
- Prices: Dropping

Vibe: Quiet beauty. Parks explode in golds and oranges. Early sunsets push everything indoors again.

Insider Tips:

1. Head to Tallinn's Telliskivi Creative City for bookstores, design shops, and warm cafés.
2. Riga's central market becomes a wonderland of root vegetables and foraged mushrooms.
3. Pack waterproof shoes — sudden rain isn't uncommon.

November

- Crowds: Dead quiet
- Temps: 0°C to 6°C (32°F to 43°F)
- Prices: Bottom of the barrel

Vibe: Moody. Great time for introspective travelers and foggy photography walks.

Insider Tips:

1. Use this month to explore indoor culture: Riga's Art Nouveau Museum, Tallinn's KUMU Art Museum, Vilnius' Church of St. Peter & Paul.
2. Cafés become second homes — you'll get to know baristas by name.
3. Fewer English speakers around — time to test out those phrasebook pages.

December

- Crowds: Medium, spike after mid-month
- Temps: -4°C to 1°C (25°F to 34°F)
- Prices: Rising around Christmas

Vibe: Holiday lights, Christmas markets, mulled wine. Festive without being frantic.

Insider Tips:

1. Riga claims Europe's first-ever Christmas tree was erected here in 1510 — check the plaque near House of the Blackheads.
2. Tallinn's Christmas Market at Town Hall Square is postcard-perfect.
3. Book your accommodations early December for the best combo of charm and chill.

Pro Moves: Smart Crowd Management

1. **Track Cruise Ships:** Especially for Tallinn. Cruise ship = street congestion. Plan Old Town visits early morning or late evening.
2. **Use the Shoulder Months:** May and September are golden. Everything's open, weather's decent, and crowds are bearable.
3. **Split Your Stay:** Don't base in just one capital. Spend 3 days in each — the rhythm shift alone gives you a deeper feel for the region.

4. **Get Out Early:** The best photo light (and empty alleys) is before 8am in summer.

Important Addresses, Emergency Contacts & Traveler Resources

You never want to need this section. But when you do, it's the most important page in your guide. I've gathered the absolute essentials here—from embassy numbers to late-night pharmacies—so you can navigate any surprise with calm and confidence. Bookmark this part before you even land.

Emergency Numbers (EU-wide standard)

One thing that's reassuring about the Baltics: they follow the European emergency standard. Wherever you are in Vilnius, Riga, or Tallinn:

Dial 112 for Police, Ambulance, or Fire services.

It connects to multilingual operators and dispatchers 24/7.

No need to look for separate numbers unless you're dealing with specific embassies, lost passports, or travel documents.

Hospitals & Clinics (Open to Travelers)

Each Baltic capital has modern hospitals—many with English-speaking staff and walk-in travel clinics.

Vilnius

Vilnius University Hospital Emergency Department

- Santariškių g. 2, Vilnius
- +370 5 236 5000
- GPS: 54.735500, 25.269308
- Open 24/7

Tip: Bring your passport and insurance card (digital copies accepted).

Medica Clinic (Private, English-speaking)

- Lukšio g. 3, Vilnius
- +370 616 58800
- Appointment usually within 2 hours.

Riga

Pauls Stradiņš Clinical University Hospital (Emergency)

- Pilsoņu iela 13, Riga
- +371 6706 9444
- GPS: 56.943521, 24.036728

ARS Medical Centre (Private, Walk-in accepted)

- Skolas iela 5, Riga
- +371 6720 0770
- Fast testing and GP access. Ask for English-speaking staff.

Tallinn

North Estonia Medical Centre (PERH)

- Sütiste tee 19, Tallinn
- +372 617 1300
- GPS: 59.407482, 24.712279
- Has international patient desk.

Confido Medical Centre

- Veerenni 51, Tallinn
- +372 629 0000
- Trusted for quick, English-speaking care.

Traveler Note:

Bring travel insurance (digital or paper), a photo ID, and know your hotel address. If you're uninsured, ER visits cost €50–€200+ depending on treatment. Private clinics often take credit cards.

Embassies & Consulates (Top Nationalities)

Here are the primary embassies for English-speaking travelers. For passport issues, arrests, medical emergencies, or legal aid, these are your lifelines:

In Vilnius:

U.S. Embassy in Lithuania

- Akmenų g. 6, Vilnius
- +370 5 266 5500
- https://lt.usembassy.gov

UK Embassy

- Antakalnio g. 2, Vilnius
- +370 5 246 2900
- https://www.gov.uk/world/lithuania

In Riga:

U.S. Embassy in Latvia

- Samnera Velsa iela 1, Riga
- +371 6710 7000
- https://lv.usembassy.gov

British Embassy

- J. Alunāna iela 5, Riga
- +371 6777 4700

In Tallinn:

U.S. Embassy in Estonia

- Kentmanni 20, Tallinn
- +372 668 8100
- https://ee.usembassy.gov

UK Embassy

- Wismari 6, Tallinn
- +372 667 4700

Insider Tip:

Embassies can't pay your hospital bill, but they can help you get a temporary passport or connect with legal counsel. Keep digital copies of your documents on a secure cloud app (Google Drive, Dropbox, etc.).

Pharmacies (Apothekas) with Extended Hours

In the Baltics, not all pharmacies are open 24/7. But these ones actually are.

Vilnius

- EuroVaistinė – Gedimino Ave 18
- Open 24h
- GPS: 54.6890, 25.2787

Riga

- Mēness Aptieka – Brīvības iela 68
- Open 24h
- GPS: 56.9617, 24.1250
- Ask for English assistance if needed.

Tallinn

- Tõnismäe Südameapteek – Pärnu mnt 10
- Open 24h
- GPS: 59.4307, 24.7465

You'll find basics like painkillers, antihistamines, and travel sickness pills OTC. But antibiotics require a local doctor's prescription—even for recurring conditions.

Traveler Resource Centers & Lost & Found

Vilnius Tourist Info Center

- Pilies g. 2, Vilnius
- +370 5 262 6470
- https://www.vilnius-tourism.lt

Riga Tourist Info Center

- Rātslaukums 6, Riga
- +371 6703 7900
- https://www.liveriga.com

Tallinn Tourist Info Center

- Niguliste 2, Tallinn
- +372 645 7777
- https://www.visittallinn.ee

Lost your phone? Bag? Check the city police Lost Property departments, but don't expect miracles without a serial number or tracker.

Pro Moves: Smart Travel Safety Strategies

- Register your trip with your home government (STEP for Americans, FCDO for Brits)
- Screenshot embassy & insurance contacts and save them offline
- Download offline maps (Google Maps or Maps.me) for the city centers
- Set up emergency contacts in your phone with a local SIM
- Pack a tiny laminated card with your hotel name/address in local language
- Carry a translated medical note if you have allergies or chronic conditions

From setting up your SIM card to knowing where to go in an emergency, this appendix isn't just filler—it's the confidence kit you carry in your back pocket. Because exploring Vilnius, Riga, and Tallinn without stress is the real freedom of no-crowd travel.

📍 GPS Disclaimer

All GPS coordinates included in this guide are accurate as of early 2025. They're intended to bring you as close as possible to entrances, parking areas, or the main landmarks—not necessarily the exact doorstep of every venue. Urban development, construction, or temporary rerouting might affect access points. Use them as your smart starting point, and double-check locations with an updated map app like Google Maps, Apple Maps, or organic sources like local signage and staff.

Image Attribution links

- https://commons.wikimedia.org/wiki/File:Vilnius_Land marks_170.jpg
- https://commons.wikimedia.org/wiki/File:Riga_Landmar ks_98.jpg
- https://commons.wikimedia.org/wiki/File:Vilnius_Land marks_30.jpg
- https://commons.wikimedia.org/wiki/File:Baltic_Coast_ Trail_(May-June_2019,_Latvia)_- _318_(49991637687).jpg
- https://commons.wikimedia.org/wiki/File:Vana_foor_Ba lti_jaamas.jpg
- https://commons.wikimedia.org/wiki/File:Akmuo_vokie %C4%8Di%C5%B3_kareiviams,_Rokoniai.JPG
- https://commons.wikimedia.org/wiki/File:Vilnius_Vilnia _2.jpg
- https://commons.wikimedia.org/wiki/File:Vilnius,_Gedi mino_prospektas_40.jpg
- https://commons.wikimedia.org/wiki/File:Maskavas_For %C5%A1tate,_Latgale_Suburb,_Riga,_Latvia_- _panoramio_(47).jpg
- https://commons.wikimedia.org/wiki/File:Kr%C4%81sla va,_L%C4%81%C8Dpl%C4%93%C5%A1a_iela_- _panoramio.jpg
- https://commons.wikimedia.org/wiki/File:L%C4%81%C4 %8Dpl%C4%93%C5%A1a_iela_-_panoramio_(2).jpg
- https://commons.wikimedia.org/wiki/File:LithuaniaHisto ry.png

- https://commons.wikimedia.org/wiki/File:OpenStreetMap_Riga_2010.png
- https://commons.wikimedia.org/wiki/File:Tallinn_overview.png
- https://commons.wikimedia.org/wiki/File:Lahemaa_Viru_bog_10.jpg
- https://commons.wikimedia.org/wiki/File:Tallinn,_Kalamaja_kalmistu.jpg
- https://commons.wikimedia.org/wiki/File:Tallinn_kohvik_Maiasmokk.jpg
- https://commons.wikimedia.org/wiki/File:Baltic_Shuttle_Bus_in_Estonia.jpg
- https://commons.wikimedia.org/wiki/File:Latvie%C5%A1u_Ziemassv%C4%93tku_%C4%93dieni.jpg
- https://commons.wikimedia.org/wiki/File:Mulgikapsad.jpg
- https://commons.wikimedia.org/wiki/File:Cepelinai_Sauce.JPG
- https://commons.wikimedia.org/wiki/File:Capital_of_Culture_Vilnius_2009,_Lawn_of_Relaxation.jpg

Back Cover Image Link attribution

- https://commons.wikimedia.org/wiki/File:Panorama_du_centre_de_Riga_(Lettonie).jpg

Map of Lithuania

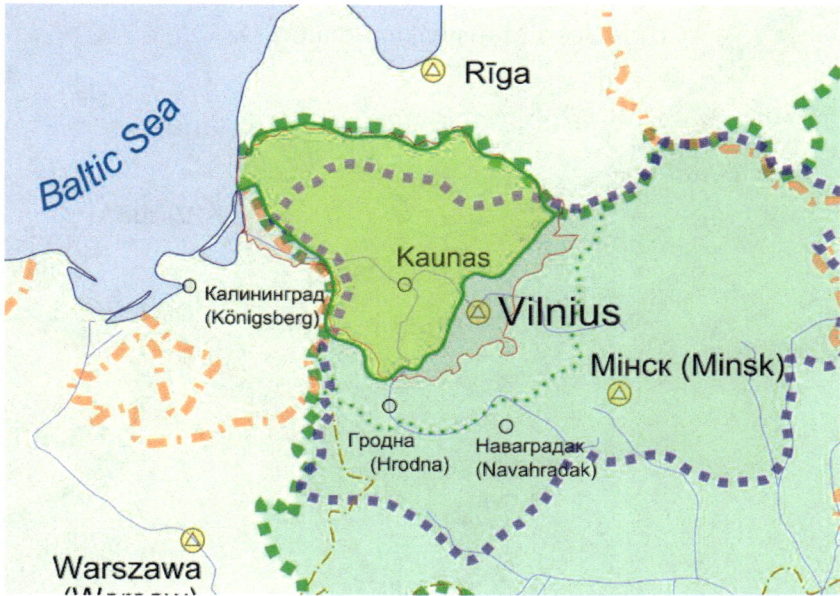

https://upload.wikimedia.org/wikipedia/commons/c/c4/Lit

Note: Click the link Above or Scan the QR Code Below to View the Map Better

Tallinn Tram Map

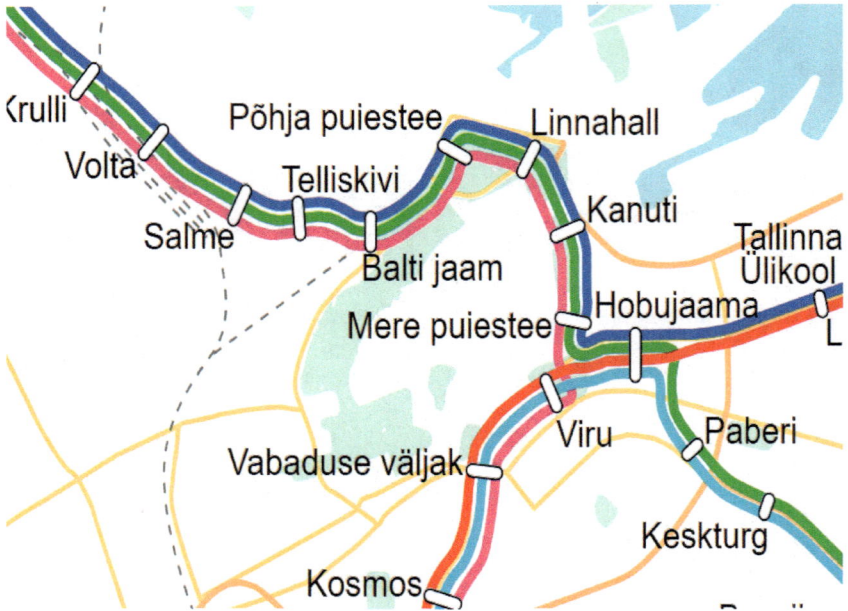

Krulli
Volta
Põhja puiestee
Linnahall
Telliskivi
Salme
Kanuti
Balti jaam
Tallinna Ülikool
Mere puiestee
Hobujaama
L
Viru
Paberi
Vabaduse väljak
Keskturg
Kosmos

Note: Click the link Above or Scan the QR Code Below To View the Map Better

Riga District Map

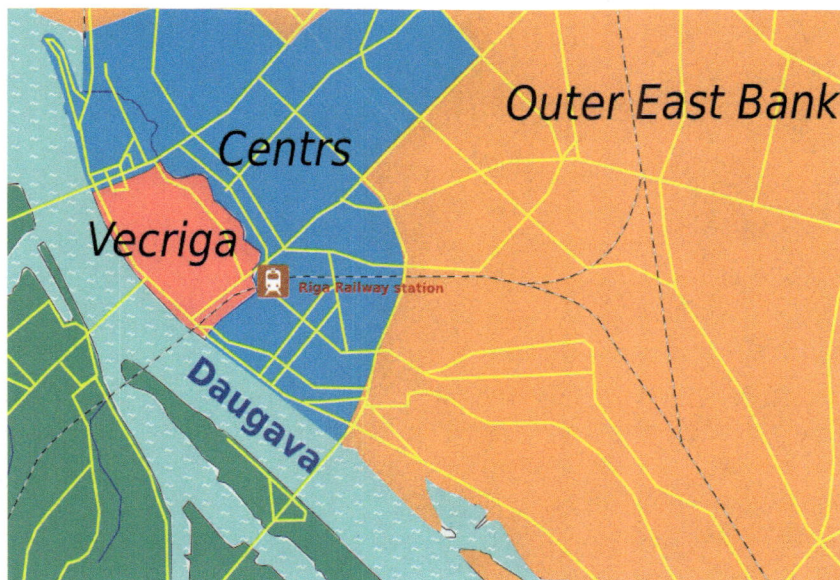

https://upload.wikimedia.org/wikipedia/commons/d/d4/Wi

Note: Click the link Above or Scan the QR Code Below to View the Map Better

Printed in Dunstable, United Kingdom

66316434R00077